4-30

.80

MARRIAGE

Duet or Discord?

MARRIAGE

Duet or Discord?

JOHN W. DRAKEFORD

ZONDERVAN PUBLISHING HOUSE
Grand Rapids

Marriage: Duet or Discord?
Formerly published under the title:
THE HOME: LABORATORY OF LIFE

A ZONDERVAN PAPERBACK — 1970
Copyright © 1965 by Broadman Press,
copyright transferred to John W. Drakeford
Second printing 1971
Dewey Decimal Classification: 301:42

Library of Congress Catalog Card No. 72-133350

Printed in the United States of America

To my two sons
Warwick
and
Brenton
teachers of the art of family living
who in the process have put
gray hairs in my head
bills in my pocket
illustrations in my sermons
happiness in my home
and pride in my heart

Contents

1. The Home: Laboratory of Life . . . 11

2. A Kiss and Its Consequences . . . 21

3. The Developing Love Life . . . 30

4. Sex—Sinful or Sacred? . . . 47

5. Marriage—Duet or Discord? . . . 60

6. Ruth, the Daughter-in-Law . . . 71

7. Facts of Life for Fathers . . . 82

8. The Family Meal . . . 94

9. Church and Family—Allies or Enemies? . . . 105

10. The Mobile Family . . . 115

Appendix . . . 127

Preface

Whatever might be the shortcomings of these sermons, they at least have two virtues: they came to birth in the processes of involvement with family relationships, and they grew to maturity as they were formulated and verbalized before groups of people.

For several years now, hours of each week have been occupied with listening to the aspirations and hopes, the expressions of frustration, disappointment, and disillusionment of men and women, husbands and wives, parents and children, boys and girls. The Baptist Marriage and Family Counseling Center, carried on as a part of the research and teaching program of the School of Religious Education of Southwestern Baptist Seminary, has provided an unparalleled opportunity for studying the "living human document" within the setting of family life.

Counseling experiences presented a diverse variety of problems of home and family life which tantalized my mind and sent me scurrying to the literature on the subject. In the process, sermons, talks, and lectures leaped out and demanded verbalization. Numerous invitations came from Parent Teacher Associations, church groups, and conferences. As I spoke on these subjects and entered into the discussion periods which followed, I became aware of the high level of interest. Here was an area of intense human need!

Working with "sick" marriages deepened the conviction of the absolute necessity for a widespread program of family life education. I gradually moved into the field until I found almost all my public ministry devoted to home and family life education, in which the experiences of the clinic could be used to reinforce the concept of the Christian home.

Realizing that part of the problem lay in the many activities of good institutions which impinge on family life, I determined my family life conferences would not compound the problem. Thus developed the Weekend Christian Home Emphasis, which involves activities on Friday evening, Saturday, and Sunday. (See appendix of this volume for a typical program.) This type of program has been conducted in churches across the southwestern United States.

The responses to the program have exceeded my most optimistic expectations and testimonials from grateful pastors, leaders of PTAs, and conference groups are very encouraging. At these conferences there are generally people who ask, "Is there any possibility of getting a copy of that message?" All too frequently my reply has been in the negative. The present volume seeks to fill the gap.

1
The Home:
Laboratory of Life

Hear, O Israel: the Lord our God is one Lord; and thou shalt love the Lord thy God with all thine heart, and with all thy soul, and with all thy might. And these words, which I command thee this day, shall be in thine heart: and thou shalt teach them diligently unto thy children, and shalt talk of them when thou sittest in thine house, and when thou walkest by the way, and when thou liest down, and when thou risest up. And thou shalt bind them for a sign upon thine hand, and they shall be as frontlets between thine eyes. And thou shalt write them upon the posts of thy house, and on thy gates (Deut. 6:4–9).

The book of Deuteronomy is Moses' farewell address. The great, old man has led the children of Israel through all their varied experiences in the wilderness. They are at last preparing to enter the long-looked-for Promised Land. Moses will not go with them, but before he leaves he wants to remind them of the way God has led and the lessons they have learned, which will prepare them for a new era of national life.

The godly leader had many things to discuss with his people. The record of these discussions became a treasure house of religious truth to which the Jewish people often referred. In his temptation experiences Jesus answered the tempter, "It is written," and then he quoted from the book of Deuteronomy.

To change from a group of wanderers in the desert to a well-ordered and settled nation presented many difficulties. Moses, trying to make a basic emphasis, highlights the role of the family in the development of national life. He also accents the interrelationships of family members in learning the skills of living and the necessity for the family to listen for the voice of God.

Relationship Between National and Family Life

Deuteronomy 5 contains the message of Moses as he recapitulated the Ten Commandments given by God to the children of Israel. One of the commandments has a special meaning and is said by Paul to be "the first commandment with promise" (Eph. 6:2).

When I was a Primary, I imagined that this commandment meant that children who honored their father and mother would live to a ripe old age—that the secret of longevity lay in being obedient to one's parents. However, some thoughtful Bible scholars see the promise as applying rather to Israel's national life. If the Israelites honored their parents and built the solid foundations of family life, they would also in the process build a strong national life. The experience of Judaism has shown the truth of the Mosaic assertion. Possibly no group of people has exalted the family as much, and at the same time retained their racial and national distinctives, as have the Jews.

Plato said that the life of the nation is only "the life of the family writ large." History has shown that the determined efforts to change the trend of national life have been associated with a consequent attitude toward the family. When ancient Sparta turned toward a military dictatorship the first step was the elimination of the family unit. Men and women lived in separate barracks, while the children were reared under the supervision of the state and trained to be loyal to the state and the state alone.

Hitler's Germany, building its Fascist system glorifying a dictator, threw away the structure of family life and passed over to the state many of the functions normally the property of the family. The dictatorial state could not bear to have a democratic family.

The most determined attempt in modern times to destroy the family has come with the advent of communism. Communism has a series of aims which can be summarized as: to dethrone God by showing that he is not only unnecessary but a mere superstition; debase man to the status of an animal; deny the Judaeo-Christian ethic by throwing out all ideas of eternal values; destroy the family and ultimately dominate the world. Destruction of the family is an essential step in the process.

In the *Communist Manifesto* the authors, Marx and Engels, pour out their scorn on the accepted ideas of the family and lay down their fundamental premise for a Communist regime—"We replace home education with social." National life and family life are so closely linked in the minds of the Communist theorists that they claim, with the new dictatorial form of society which they will inaugurate, the family will vanish. However, as communism came into power it did not wait for the family to vanish. It translated theory into practice and did everything it could to undermine the solidarity of the family unit.

Communism's success in attaining its objective may be

seen in the happenings under a Communist rule in China. China has a strong tradition emphasizing the family. Despite this, however, the regime has been able to set up its communes. People's lives are strictly regulated, even to the amount of food which may be consumed; and the basic family loyalties, once so characteristic of the Chinese, have been broken down to give the all-powerful state mastery of the situation.

In America we honor the family and see it as a basic and fundamental unit of society. Love is serenaded and more people than ever enter into a marriage relationship. But the picture is not really as rosy as it might first appear. Elton Trueblood jars us when he says that what the Communists are doing of a deliberate intent and purpose we are unwittingly doing, for American families are in trouble. The family is being abolished not by decree but by the erosion of a thousand forces. With almost one out of every three marriages falling apart we must face the inevitable repercussions on the strength of our national life.

The challenge is to focus more attention on the home. Patriots, in the best sense of the word, will make a significant step in their patriotic duty when they bend their energies to strengthen family life. It is a peculiar Christian responsibility. The church can minister to the family in a manner that no other institution can and we must accept our responsibilities.

> So long as there are homes to which men turn
>   At the close of day,
> So long as there are homes where children are—
>   Where women stay,
> If love and loyalty and faith be found
>   Across these sills,

A stricken nation can recover from
  Its gravest ills.

So long as there are homes where fires burn
  And there is bread,
So long as there are homes where lamps are lit
  And prayers are said;
Although people falter through the dark
  And nations grope,
With God himself inside these little homes
  We still can hope.[1]

Religion in the Home

Educators differ in their evaluation of the best teaching techniques. Some have maintained that no matter how we theorize, there is a certain body of knowledge which must be imparted, and the passing on of that knowledge is the main task of the teacher. This has sometimes been called the "material-centered" approach. In contrast stands the group who claim that learning takes place through activity and experience. As an individual participates he becomes involved in life's experiences—he comes to understand and assimilate the lessons to be learned.

Our text assumes a certain truth to be taught, "Hear, O Israel: The Lord our God is one Lord: . . . thou shalt love the Lord thy God with all thine heart, and with all thy soul, and with all thy might." Jesus called this the first and greatest of all the commandments, and went on to add that there was one like it, "Thou shalt love thy neighbour as thyself." Summed up in these two state-

---

[1] From *Light of the Years* by Grace Noll Crowell. Copyright by Harper & Brothers. Reprinted by permission of Harper & Row, Publishers, Inc.

ments are all the basic loyalties of an individual to both God and man.

Giving emphasis to the place of teaching, Moses says, "Thou shalt teach them diligently." Even without using the word "diligent" repetition would still be implied, for the Hebrew word translated "teach" literally means "to whet," to sharpen. The illusion is to a man's using a knife. He sharpens it, but as he works its cutting edge is removed and resharpening is necessary if it is to remain an effective tool. It is never safe to assume any lesson has been taught, for teaching is a constant and unending process.

The activity aspect is referred to by Moses when he says the parents must talk of these words to their children when "thou sittest in thine house, and when thou walkest by the way, and when thou liest down, and when thou risest up." All the activities of home life were to be the media through which the divine truth was to be taught. See the little boy as he sits on his mother's knee. She is reading him a story before he goes to bed. It is not a nursery story nor a fairy tale. She reads from a book of church history. It is small wonder that when the boy grows to be a man his mind is captivated by the thrilling history of the church, and Dr. W. W. Barnes becomes one of the greatest historians ever produced by Southern Baptists.

If the teaching was to be effective these words were to become a part of the parents' lives. These words . . . shall be in thine heart, and thou shalt bind them for a sign upon thine hand, and they shall be as frontlets between thine eyes. . . . Thou shalt write them upon the posts of thy house, and on thy gates." But how were these commandments followed? The Jews developed phylacteries—small containers having verses of Scripture within them. These containers were tied on their hands and on their forehead. They constructed a mezuzah, which had within it a small passage of Scripture, and nailed it to the doorpost of the house. Thus, they felt that they had literally fulfilled the divine commandment passed on by Moses.

But what was the probable intent of the commandment of Moses? It does not seem meant to be taken literally. Fastening the word of God in the frontlets between the eyes probably meant that every thought was to be governed by the Word of God. Binding verses of Scripture on the hand seemed to indicate that every act was to be in conformity with the Word of God. Writing the Scripture verse on the doorposts and the gates of the house surely meant that there was to be a godly atmosphere and that the Word of God was to permeate the whole house.

The ancient Mosaic emphasis has been verified by modern sociologists. The home is the laboratory of life! The experiences one has within the family prepare him for social encounters he will have in the wider circles of life. Within the family are possibilities of an infinite variety of interpersonal experiences. An application of the mathematical *law of interaction* to family life shows that if two members are in a family there is only one relationship possible, but if there are eight members in the family twenty-eight possible relationships present themselves. The give-and-take within family life provides social experiences which will determine, in a large measure, the type of adults the children will become.

Family life reveals aspects of personality often unnoticed in other processes of life. Marriage counselors often advise young people to go and stay in their prospective partner's home for a week or so and watch the behavior of their loved one. The way he behaves in the family setting and the attitudes he has toward the other members of the family will probably show the pattern of his normal, everyday behavior and indicate the way he will react toward his partner in future family experiences.

Most emphasis is laid on the responsibility of the parents within the family. In verse 20, the son asks his father, "What mean the testimonies, and the statutes, and the judgments, which the Lord our God hath commanded you?" Put this into a modern setting and imagine a father's reading the paper or watching his favorite television show. His son approaches and asks, "What mean the testimonies, and the statutes, and the judgments, which the Lord our God hath commanded you?" The father looks up, startled, and says, "What on earth are you talking about?" The son repeats the question and the father says, "Goodness only knows, why come and worry me? Go ask the preacher or your Sunday school teacher!"

Modern parents have become adept at the art of delegating. We send our children to school to get their education, to the library to get their books, to the park to get their recreation, to the movies for their entertainment, and to the church for their religion. But there are some responsibilities which cannot be delegated. These belong fairly and squarely upon the shoulders of the parents. The teaching of religion is one such responsibility.

Religion is *caught* as well as *taught*. An outstanding American preacher tells how much he hated math in high school and how he determined that when he went to college he would avoid every math course at any cost. At college he met a faculty member to whom he was attracted and as their friendship grew, to his horror he discovered that his older friend was the math professor. His whole attitude toward math changed and he finally ended up taking every math course available. Within the family circle the interpersonal relationships with parents will do more in the process of teaching religion than any amount of formal study.

What God Wants

The commandment which Moses passed on to his people was, "Thou shalt love the Lord thy God." The word for love is that which is generally used for family life. It is used for loving God on only three occasions: in the Decalogue, Deborah's song, and here. In the book of Hosea it is used to tell of the love which a husband had for his unfaithful wife. It is also used to describe a father's love for his son.

We might say in effect that God is telling us he wants our love, but it is to be the sort of love that we have for our fellowmen. It is not just some special faculty given to a favored few. It is the capacity to love which we have and which we exercise within our family group.

We should particularly note the phrase, "Hear, O Israel," which is mentioned so many times in the Old Testament. God calls for a response. He does not bludgeon his way into an individual's life. Before a covenant relationship can come into existence between God and a family, each family member must be individually prepared to listen to the voice of God.

A husband and wife lived happily together for many

years. Then a strange barrier began to grow between them. The wife withdrew and finally looked at her husband with unknowing eyes. Reluctantly he took her to a doctor who in turn referred them to a psychiatrist. The psychiatrist committed her to a sanitarium for treatment. Week by week the husband continued to visit her, but as he sat and tried to make conversation, she gave no hint of ever having known him. One day the psychiatrist advised the husband to take his wife back to the town where they had grown up, in the hope that some familiar scene might jar a memory and help the process of recovery.

Back in the old town they wandered around the streets redolent with childhood memories. They walked across the fields and down to the little stream where barefooted they waded through the waters. Later as they sat on the bank she lay back and dropped off to sleep. At long last she opened her eyes and, for the first time in months, there was recognition, as she asked, "Jim! Jim, where have you been all this time?"

Her husband lovingly took her hand in his and replied, "Honey, I haven't been anywhere, I've been right beside you, waiting for you to awaken and become aware of my presence."

God is right beside each one of us. In him we live and move and have our being. He loves us with an everlasting love that calls us to respond. The family relationship can and should show us what this love means.

2
A Kiss
and Its Consequences

Jacob kissed Rachel, and lifted up his voice, and wept (Gen. 29:11).

The stories of the Bible come from a dry and arid land. As a result of the perpetual water shortage, the availability of the precious liquid determined the fertility and prosperity of the countryside. The never-ending search for sources of water was sometimes rewarded with the discovery of a spring, making the surrounding area much sought after real estate. The surest way to hamstring an enemy was to stop up his well and cut off his water supply.

In the conflict with Isaac, the Philistines filled in the wells which his father had dug, and one of Isaac's most notable achievements was that he "digged again the wells of water, which they had digged in the days of Abraham his father" (Gen. 26:18).

As wells were discovered, the surrounding area blossomed as the rose; and the oasis of lush vegetation glistened like a green emerald in a setting of desert gold. Towns followed with houses like frightened chickens gathered around a hen in close proximity to the life-giving supply of water.

Social life in a Palestinian town often centered around the well. Waiting to draw water, women fell into conversation, as the news and events of the town were swapped. One of the most meaningful of all the discourses of Jesus was given to the woman of Samaria, as she drew water from a well.

The locale of our text is by a well. Jacob, fleeing as a fugitive from his father's wrath, came into Haran, looking for his Uncle Laban. Shepherds clustered at the well were waiting for the opportunity to water their sheep. So Jacob asked them concerning Laban. In response they pointed to the attractive girl leading a flock of sheep toward the very spot where they stood. She was Rachel, the daughter of Laban, and she was beautiful and well-favored. Attraction gave speed to Jacob's feet as he hurried to the well to help water her sheep. At the conclusion of his pleasant chore, "Jacob kissed Rachel, and lifted up his voice, and wept."

Why did Jacob lift up his voice and weep? He might more appropriately have picked up a sheep in each arm, or in gay abandon wrestled with a herdsman, or leapt across the mouth of the well, or made some other joyous gesture. But he wept.

He may have had prophetic insight. That kiss was to cost him. He worked for seven years for Rachel. Then on the wedding day he lifted his bride's veil to discover that he had her sister Leah. He had to work yet another seven years for Rachel.

Although a kiss can be an exhilarating experience, it may have a disappointing sequel.—Jacob kissed Rachel. How simple and romantic it all sounds! But kisses have a strange knack of being the forerunners of other experiences.

A poet has said, "A kiss should be felt and the least

said about it the better." However, despite this suggestion, something needs to be said on the subject.

During World War II, two young people were walking through a London street when the air raid warning sounded. They hurried to a crowded air raid shelter and as they stood closely packed together, the lights went out. When they came on again, the young lady stood blushing and said to her boy friend, "Oh Herbert, you shouldn't have done it."

"Shouldn't have done what?" queried Herbert.

"You shouldn't have kissed me when the lights went out."

Herbert looked at her with amazement and said, "I didn't kiss you." Then, as he gazed belligerently around, he said, "I wish I could catch the man who did. I'd teach him."

"Oh Herbert," she replied, "you couldn't teach him anything."

In the Bible, as in all of life, there are many different kinds of kisses. It is not so much the kiss as the intent that counts. The kiss which is a part of the flamboyant embrace of a maiden aunt is different from the protesting grimace of a small child, and the kiss of a lover is different from either.

As difficult as the situation of Jacob and Rachel was, it was easy compared with the problems faced by modern young people. The young people of that day lived their lives under the watchful eyes of guardians, and their society expected them to be discreet in all their contacts with each other.

The kiss between the sexes of the age of Jacob and Rachel is part of a response which is a preliminary to further sexual experience. With many young people today who are biologically ready for marriage but are not prepared educationally, vocationally, or financially, abundant sex urges find their outlet in "necking" or "petting."

Even if Jacob and Rachel managed to slip away from the tents of their parents, they still did not have the dubious benefits of the automobile. Like the camel of Jacob's day, the automobile is meant to be a means of transportation, but it has become much more than that. For many young people it has become a status symbol, a bar, a meeting place. Moreover, a Jacob and a Rachel could hardly do much necking on a camel, but the car has become a love nest, providing unparalleled opportunities for illicit sexual experiences. One study of unwed mothers showed the biggest proportion of them had their sexual experiences in automobiles.

Because there is greater freedom for young people, more sexual stimulation on every side from the entertainment media, and an infinite variety of opportunities for petting, a young person of this day must be more mature and able to face up to the implications of what is involved in the experience. Dr. Popenoe has suggested a number of questions which may serve as criteria by which to evaluate a petting experience.

1. Does it mean the same to both of you, or is one callously exploiting the other to get a feeling of power, or a cheap thrill?
2. Is it primarily physical, or does it involve the total personality?
3. Is it unaesthetic, deceitful, furtive, shamefaced, or is it open, sincere, honest, and wholehearted?
4. Does it interfere with other (more) important activities?

5. Is it (like) a habit-forming drug, of which larger and larger amounts are required to produce the same effect?

6. Is it a satisfying fulfillment of life at its best; or does it leave one feeling wrought up, dissatisfied, frustrated?

7. Is it preparation for future married life? [1]

Love play is a preliminary to sexual relationships and preliminaries continually carried on without consummation bring tremendous strains. A young man hoped to learn to fly an airplane. A friend who owned a plane agreed to let him climb over it and practice operating the controls. As he sat in the cockpit, practicing with the controls, he decided to start the engine to get the feel of it. While "revving up" the engine, he "revved" too long. The plane went racing down the field to crash at the end of the runway. Any marriage counselor can tell the oft-repeated tragedies of "take-offs" following too much "revving up," which not only complicate lives but brings misery and tragedy.

Prime Minister Gladstone once delivered in England's House of Commons a speech about a kiss. He told the story of Princess Alice whose small son had contracted diphtheria. The doctors had isolated him and warned his mother to stay away.

However, mother-like, she was constantly peeping in to check on her son. On one occasion the little boy saw his mother and reaching out his thin arms called, "Mommy, come and kiss me." She rushed across the room, wrapped him up in her arms, kissed him, caught the diphtheria, and died.

Gladstone's speech was to report her passing.

---

[1] Paul Popenoe, *Marriage: Before and After* (New York: Wilfred Funk, 1943), pp. 77–80.

All too tragically the kiss which promises so much can easily bring misery and sorrow.

> Alas, how easily things go wrong!
> A sigh too much, or a kiss too long,
> And there follows a mist and a weeping rain,
> And life is never the same again.

A kiss is just the first step in choosing a mate.—It could hardly be said that Jacob rushed into marriage. He worked for fourteen years to earn Rachel for his own. Their concern for the demands of Rachel's father was typical of their day.

Jacob's experiences illustrate some of the principles of the Eastern concept of courtship and marriage. Marriages were frequently arranged by the parents. After the marriage, brides could be added, traded, or exchanged. David and Vera Mace have shown that in the West the situation is complicated by the ideas of equality, freedom, independence, and fulfilment.[2]

Jacob's wife was certainly not his *equal*. He was assumed to be her master and she his subservient partner, whose main objective was to make her husband happy. The Bible refers to Sarah who obeyed Abraham, calling him lord. Today we have the fifty-fifty marriage—the union of two equals, which requires two mature equals to respond and react to each other.

Freedom was almost an unknown for women in Jacob's day. His bride had little to say about whom she would marry and this was, and still is, typical of Eastern cultures.

---

[2] *Marriage: East and West* (Garden City: Doubleday & Co., 1960), pp. 55–57.

Our culture gives young people freedom to choose a life partner and the exercise of this freedom calls for knowledge and understanding so that the freedom may be handled in a responsible way.

Another element mentioned by the Maces is *fulfilment*. This goes to the very heart of the problem. In marriages of the past there was very little hope that any special return would come from the experience. In our overromanticized age people all too frequently expect there will be some gain coming to them when they are married so they will become different people. Marriage in reality is not so much a matter of getting as of giving. If it is to be successful one has to give more than he gets.

Even in Jacob's day there were elements of unreality about his courting experience. The writer says, "Jacob served seven years for Rachel; and they seemed unto him but a few days, for the love he had to her" (Gen. 29:20). Anyone who could work for seven years and feel that it was only a few days must have been living at less than the reality level.

A kiss has been called a contraction of the lips which results from an expansion of the heart. This expansion of the heart is the root of the trouble. Emotion becomes so strong that rational processes are superseded.

There is a strange condition called "infatuation," which overtakes its victims with a remarkable suddenness. Infatuation may be defined as "an intensely emotional, generally sexual, attachment, lacking a reasonable basis, and of short duration." The elements of excessive emotionality, strong sexual overtones, lacking a reasonable basis, and of short duration make infatuation an experience in which the elements necessary for a stable marriage are lacking.

Despite the skeptical statement of a teen-ager who said, "If your parents approve they think it is love, if they disapprove they think it is just infatuation," there is still a distinction between love and infatuation. Unfortunately, there are no simple scientific criteria for choosing a partner. The following suggestions may offer help in the choice of a partner for life.

Make sure you are both old enough. Ideas change with passing time. The boy who is so "cute" at seventeen may seem to be only a fool when you are twenty-five. Young people, anxious to get away from their parents, often find to their dismay that an early marriage only throws them back into their parents' arms, for "he who pays the piper calls the tune." Very few real early marriages can manage without some kind of parental subsidy. The best age for marriage is somewhere in the early or middle twenties. Early marriages can succeed, but the partners must work harder to make them go.

Get to know your prospective partner. Some writers claim it takes approximately two years to get to know another person. Take time, for there is all of life ahead. Don't just see him when he takes you out on a date. See him at home, spend some time with his folks and watch his reactions to them, for that is the way he'll probably react to you later. The old saying, "Marry in haste and repent at leisure," is still valid.

Anticipate marrying someone who is something like yourself. You and your partner should be pretty close to the same age. If the difference is too great it will cause difficulties. The future bride or groom should be from about the same socioeconomic level. It is all right to dream about the millionaire's son who will woo and win you, but it will probably be someone on your own socioeconomic level and with whom you would be much more compatible. You will certainly need someone with the same religious convictions.

There are some people who think a kiss can accomplish almost anything. The pastor of a church in Florida took me out fishing with a very gifted fisherman. In a boat near us was a young couple also fishing. While I was landing a fish my two friends burst into laughter. When I asked the reason for their merriment, they told me that the young couple had kissed and, just as they kissed, each hooked a fish. "That might be what it takes," I commented. Whereupon my preacher friend replied, "Well, I don't care if I never get a fish, I'm not going to kiss you."

Kisses won't catch fish. While they may help you catch a boy or girl friend, it will take more than kisses to make a marriage really function.

3
The Developing Love Life

When I was a child, I spake as a child, I felt as a child, I thought as a child: now that I am become a man, I have put away childish things. . . . Now abideth . . . love (1 Cor. 13: 11–13, ASV).

It was once my privilege to sit under a great banyan tree in Honolulu, where Robert Louis Stevenson had sat and written many years before. As I gazed at the spread of that giant tree, my thoughts were of that great writer. Late in life, with his health failing, Stevenson went to the South Sea Islands to live. Vailima, his house on the island of Samoa, was some distance from the main highway and could only be reached by a precipitous pathway. While living there, Stevenson took a great interest in the natives and tried to help them in the difficulties they encountered in adjusting to the white man's law. As a gesture of gratitude for what he had done for them, the natives got together and built a roadway to his home. They called this roadway *Ala Lota Alofa*—the Road of the Loving Heart.

There is a sense in which every individual has to climb the "road of the loving heart." It is not an easy climb. There are numerous rough spots along the way. Many people have managed it very successfully, without help from anyone, by just doing "what comes naturally." Unfortunately, many others have fallen by the way and failed miserably in their efforts.

Paul's statement, in 1 Corinthians 13, is probably the most definitive ever made on the subject of love. It is significant that as he draws his statement to a conclusion, in the words of our text, he re-emphasizes the absolute necessity of love's being a growth experience.

Levels of Love

Any discussion of love faces the difficulty of definition. The problem of semantics has never loomed larger. People speak of loving such dissimilar objects as God, pecan pie, cats, old shoes, money, and mother. Surely they do not mean the same thing when they speak about these different objects.

The difficulty is that our English word covers so many different ideas. The Greek language, with its three words for love, opens the possibility of a closer categorization. *Eros*, *philia*, and *agape*, translated love, can serve as a basis for definition, although even in the Greek the meanings are not always as precise as may be indicated here.

Eros, or selfish love, is that basic physical attraction between the sexes. The individual who experiences such love hopes to gain some release or expression from it. It is significant that this word is nowhere mentioned in the New Testament.

Sex and love are not necessarily the same and such widely separated writers as Reik and Duvall have shown that often they can be the antithesis of each other. Nevertheless, there is a physical, sexual basis to human love, which can act like steel and concrete to build a strong, solid marriage relationship.

Philia may be thought of as the mental level of love—the attraction of two similar intellectual and cultural interests. *Philia* is used in the New Testament. J. B. Phillips indicates the difference between *philia* and *agape* in his translation of Jesus' confrontation with his discredited disciple after the resurrection. "When they had finished breakfast Jesus said to Simon Peter, 'Simon, son of Jonah, do you love [*agape*] me more than those others?'

" 'Yes, Lord,' he replied, 'you know that I am your friend [*philia*]' " (John 21:15–16).

Some of the classical love affairs of history were on the *philia* level. The experience of Robert Browning's keeping up his correspondence with Elizabeth Barrett, a spinster in her late thirties, living as an invalid and postponing the day of meeting, was mainly *philia*. A marriage built on sexual attraction alone will have little to give it permaaanance and stability. The similarity of outlook on life, however, will help to smooth the way for an enduring relationship.

Agape is the altruistic level of love. It is the great rich word of the New Testament predominantly used to describe the love of God toward men and that which Christians are to have for each other. The altruistic or unselfish note is characteristic of *agape*. Paul sets it out in all its glory in 1 Corinthians 13, where there is a constant refrain of the altruistic attitude of love:

This love of which I speak is slow to lose patient—it looks for a way of being constructive. It is not possessive: it is neither anxious to impress nor does it cherish inflated ideas of its own importance.

Love has good manners and does not pursue selfish advantage. It is not touchy. It does not keep account of evil or gloat over the wickedness of other people (vv. 4–7).[1]

When compared with the literature of antiquity on the subject, Paul's exposition is like a towering mountain in a desert of wasteland. The main differentiating point in Paul's portrayal is that of unselfishness. We should note, however, that love cannot just be split into three segments. With the possible exception of *eros*, the levels of love are not necessarily exclusive of each other. There is an interplay of all in most expressions of love.

The Nature of Love

Having faced the complexities of the definition of love, we are immediately confronted with an equally difficult task when we come to describe the nature of love. Three features of love which are not at all obvious but must be kept in mind in our considerations are that love is reciprocal, object-seeking, and mobile.

Reciprocal aspects of love must be stressed if one of the worst features of romantic love is to be countered. All too frequently a girl feels she is waiting for a knight in shining armor who will come riding along on his white horse, see some unusual features about this attractive creature, fall in love with her, and carry her off to his castle. The stress is on being loved rather than loving. Too many people feel that "to love" is simple but "to be loved" is difficult. Erich Fromm says such an attitude comes in part from our "marketing orientation."[2] In much the same manner

---

[1] From *The New Testament in Modern English*, © J. B. Phillips, 1958. Used with permission of The Macmillan Company.
[2] *The Art of Loving* (New York: Harper & Row, 1956), p. 4.

as goods are packaged, dresses, make-up, hairdos, and all the rest are techniques to make us more "marketable," so that someone will fall in love with us.

We must learn to love before we can ever really be loved. Both aspects are important. It is essential to both love and be loved, and our love relationship is at its best when the two elements are present.

Another feature of love is its relationship to "objects." Smiley Blanton has reminded us that "love in its widest possible meaning is simply an intense, positive interest in an object."[3] The singer can enthusiastically announce, "I'm in love, I'm in love." But the listener may ask, in love with whom? The growing and developing individual focuses his love on different objects. In the long haul from infancy to maturity inappropriate objects will always be available. Failure to discern the correct object at any given stage is a constant hazard for the growing individual.

Love is mobile. In the parlance of romantic love, "falling in love" implies a condition into which an individual enters and remains henceforth. It is a static situation. Karl Menninger tries to correct the misconception when he says, "One does not 'fall' in love: one *grows* into love and love grows in him; and this begins not in adolescence nor maturity, but in infancy."[4] Love is a living, vital part of personality and, like everything else that lives, can be nourished or neglected. It is flexible and variable. Developmental factors in personality are no more significant in any area of life than in our thought about love.

---

[3] *Love or Perish* (New York: Simon & Schuster, 1956), p. 108.
[4] *Love Against Hate* (New York: Harcourt, Brace & Co., 1942), p. 261.

The mobility of love life brings its own peculiar problems. Imagine a group of people climbing the "Road of the Loving Heart" in Samoa. Some would climb a little way, see an enticing spot by the way, and decide to go no farther. Others would continue on but, when they reached a particularly difficult spot, would turn around and retreat to easier terrain. Psychologists use the word *fixation* to describe the first experience. The individual doesn't grow beyond a certain level of love. In the second experience, called *regression*, a certain level is reached but the individual is not comfortable. He has some threatening experiences and retreats to an earlier level of the love life. Fixation and regression are the enemies of a growing love life.

Love Objects

A discussion of love objects raises one of the biggest problems of any discussion on love. One writer says that "mistakes are not due to simply love or hate in themselves. We commit errors under the urgent pressure of those accumulated emotional forces, *we are driven to love or hate the wrong people, at the wrong time, for the wrong reason*." [5]

If we are to have a successful, growing love life, we must have some understanding about appropriate love objects. Love must focus on the suitable object at the appropriate time.

Self.—The infant loves himself. A newborn babe has much in common with the other forms of animal life. Its main drive is physiological. It must ingest food to grow.

---

[5] Blanton, *op. cit.*, p. 167.

A fond mother feels it is a manifestation of love when the baby snuggles into her breast, but it is truer to the facts to say he hopes to get food.

The pleasure in the infant's life comes first of all through its mouth and "oral activity" and is as necessary for the infant psychologically as it is physiologically. Oral activity and its pleasures, encountered so early in life, will remain to both enrich and bedevil the infant throughout his developing life.

The infant is the complete egotist. All of life exists to minister to him. The attitude is natural and essential in a small child but becomes inappropriate in the full-grown adult. An individual may become fixated or regress to this earlier stage of development. Thumb-sucking is a form of regression. Later it can be overeating, smoking, or some other form of oral activity. Many overweight people, psychologists believe, eat for pleasure and psychological reassurance rather than nourishment. Some of the current success of liquid diets may be due to infantile satisfaction from the milky fluid for the frustrated "fatty."

The self-centered woman, displaying her scantily clad body, spending all of her money on clothes, and dissolving into tears to get her own way, may be regressing to this earlier stage of development of the love life.

The Greeks told the tale of Narcissus who, looking into a pool, saw a reflection of himself and fell in love with his own image. Some psychologists have used the term "narcissism" to describe the preoccupation of an individual with himself.

A certain amount of self-love is essential for adequate development of the ego. But this evaluation of one's self must be made in the context of reference to other people. Jesus said, "Thou shalt love thy neighbor as thyself" (James 2:8). Cain, with his question, "Am I my brother's keeper?" (Gen. 4:9), becomes the representative of an infantile self-centeredness which is the antithesis of Christianity.

Mother.—For the infant, mother is the center of his world *physically*. She takes care of him, gives him food, and is with him most of his waking hours. The child's first *social* relationship is with his mother. She is also the center of his world *psychologically*.

Mother love, with its accompanying physical and psychological contacts, fosters adequate personality development. Rena Spitz tells of two groups of babies in institutions. The institutions were evenly matched in all ways, but one kept the babies *with* their mothers, and the other cared for them *without* the help of their mothers. In a two-year period it was shown that the children whose mothers participated developed in every way at a much more rapid rate than the others.

Of more recent days a prominent psychologist has concluded that the rhythmic heartbeat of the mother is beneficial for the child and may even serve as the basis for the child's later appreciation of music. Studying groups of babies in hospitals, an experimenter found that when the rhythmic sound of a normal heartbeat was amplified into the hospital nursery, the babies were more relaxed and gained more weight than those in a normal nursery setting.

As vital as mother love is at this stage of development, it can be fixated on this early object and life may be lived at an infantile level. The complexities of the situation are illustrated with the well-known story of the young husband who said, "You don't make biscuits the way Mother used to."

His bright young wife replied, "And you don't bring home the sort of dough that Daddy did."

Father comes into sight.—Like a man standing on the seashore watching a ship appearing on the horizon as a tiny speck and gradually growing into a distinguishable outline, the infant becomes increasingly aware of the shadowy figure of father. Finally he is delineated as a companion to the all-powerful mother figure. The experiences of relationship with a father figure will help to mold the pattern of the developing personality.

When I first started out in the ministry I had very little experience and was perplexed with many of my responsibilities. My natural reaction was to think of the way in which my home church pastor conducted his ministry. He wore a grey suit, so I wore a grey suit; he wore a black tie and so did I; he carried a New Testament in his hip pocket, and naturally I carried one in mine. In all that I tried to do I thought back to him and the way he carried out his pastoral duties.

Psychologists would say I was "identifying" with my pastor. In a similar way children identify with their parents. Boys identify with their fathers and learn to become fathers in turn. A father is important for a girl, too, for in her relationship with her father she sees the acting out of the masculine role and learns essential lessons that will be of value to her in all her relationships with the opposite sex.

What does this mean for the church? The Old Testament portrays the father as an essential figure in the teaching of religion. With the rapid breakup of marriages and the custody of the children being given to their mothers, greater numbers of children will be without father figures in their lives. Thus, a great responsibility is placed on the church and its ministry, as it seeks to provide at least some type of surrogate parent through its organization life.

Experimenters have shown that emotional bonds, rather than biological, build the relationship. Substitute parents sometimes do a better job than the biological parents.

Churches are increasingly putting men to work in close contact with young children. It is not an unusual sight to see a very masculine individual sitting with a group of tiny children. As churches enlist men and involve them in their organizational life, it may be that they will strengthen personality development. Too, this will add significance to the child's concepts of God as he learns the Model Prayer, "Our Father which art in heaven."

Playmates become important.—The growing child becomes aware of the children of his own age and sex. He enters into the "gang stage" of development. Some psychologists use the term "homosexual," implying the satisfaction coming to children from associating with their own sex. A boy, rebuked for not playing with his cousin, when asked the reason gave the simple explanation, "She's a girl." At this stage the boys prefer to be with boys and girls prefer girls. They have their own organizations and often get crushes on their leaders. Group solidarity is characteristic. Boys play at masculine games, and girls find their amusement in imitating the feminine roles of life.

Once again the activity is appropriate for the stage of

development. Fixation may lead to the tragic dilemma of homosexuality. Men who spend all their time with "the boys" or women who become so involved in their club that they do not fulfil their duties to their families may be examples of regression to this level of development of the love life.

The opposite sex takes on new significance.—Adolescence comes with explosive force. As the latent sex drive becomes overt, love objects change from homosexual to heterosexual. Half child and half adult, the adolescent is like a beginning waterskier. He struggles desperately to get up and skim along the surface of the water but frequently slips over and falls, feeling hopelessly bogged down with the futility of the effort.

The metaphor of "falling" is particularly appropriate, for possibly the most dangerous fall in adolescence is "falling in love." The strange experience overtakes its victim with alarming suddenness. In some respects it is like an attack of fever with its associated delirium. The results are longer lasting, for the victims fall in love, get married, and "live happily ever after."

Impartial observers doubt if there is such an experience. Menninger says that people don't "fall in love" but rather grow in love, and love grows in them. As for living happily ever after from this one experience, investigators claim that most normal people have about six or seven love affairs before finally taking the marital plunge.

Early adolescence is polygamous in character. Boy-girl relationships are short-lived and changes of partners frequent, a consideration which immediately raises the problem of "going steady." The craze spreads through high school, junior high, and even elementary schools. It bristles with problems. Social experiences are limited just at the time when a variety is needed. An uneven commitment may result with the girl in dead earnest and the boy taking the relationship casually or vice versa. With two adolescents constantly thrown together, and bored with the process, an emotional involvement easily ensues.

Adults must accept their share of the blame in this situation. Someone has spoken about "the plot to abolish childhood." Some parents will not let their children be children by insisting on their becoming little men and women. Thus, wittingly or unwittingly, they foster the "going steady" craze. High school marriages dramatize the dilemma. One mother plaintively put it when she said, "Before they were married we couldn't keep them apart, now that they are married we cannot keep them together." Going steady flies in the face of the polygamous nature of the early adolescent love life.

Contact with reality is a widely used criterion for the evaluation of emotional health. The desirable pathway of human development has been described as being "from pleasure to reality." If these presumptions be true, many aspects of romantic love are not only indications of emotional maladjustment but also have overtones of some type of insanity, for in its worst forms romantic love is pre-eminently unrealistic.

The lover frequently builds such an idealized picture of his beloved that the expectations could never be fulfilled by a normal human. Marriage and sex are so envisaged that they cannot possibly be attained. The emotional elements of life are exaggerated until the rational aspects are almost entirely excluded. Love becomes for many a "delicious insanity" and, like many other psychotic conditions, the road back to normality may be rough and rugged.

There are tough and difficult sections on the "Road of the Loving Heart," and adolescence probably represents the toughest pull of all. Not only is it difficult to negotiate but the roadblocks of fixation and regression never loomed larger.

The philanderer who drifts from one partner to another is still in the polygamous stage, while the individual forever looking for a "good time" may be fixated or regressed to the adolescent stage, as is the "eternal adolescent" found in every group.

Not unnaturally, too, many people who skipped the polygamous period by going steady too young, or marrying at an early age, often feel they were robbed of something in life. Dissatisfied married women will frequently lament that they never had a chance to be a girl. They feel they have been married all their lives. The developmental processes of life exact their toll when they are ignored or bypassed.

For better or for worse.—The crisis moment comes in the growing love life when one person of the opposite sex is selected as a love object and a marriage relationship is established.

Religion enters to play its part and hallow the relationship. The old Roman idea had been divorce by consent, but the Christian marriage vow says, "for better, for worse, for richer, for poorer, in sickness and in health, till death us do part." Even in its most liberal attitudes toward divorce, the church has agreed with reluctance. It has seen divorce as a surgical procedure, cutting apart a single organism which should really be one flesh.

So comes the monogamous stage of love, and it is amazing to see how casually people enter into such a lifetime commitment. Emotionality is the roadblock. With the high premium placed on emotional responses, the necessary rational processes that should be utilized in selecting a partner are bypassed.

Religion plays a vital role in marriage. It strengthens and supports an altruistic view of love by showing that true love is not earned but is best manifested in an attitude of giving. Conflicts within marriage are helped by showing that all are sinners and need forgiveness. Religion helps with the budget by putting first things first. A sense of community is engendered by the fellowship of the church with its social life and pastoral assistance. The church and the family stand as two basic institutions whose destinies are tied together.

Little hands reach out.—Although many young people do not seem to realize it, one of the logical outcomes of marriage is parenthood. In their preoccupation with each other they sometimes feel their love life has reached its climax. Pregnancy and children are viewed as intrusions into the idealistic stage and they make no preparation for commencing a family. Human nature being what it is, their plans sometimes go astray.

It certainly seems wise for a young couple to wait a year or so before starting a family, especially when the working wife can help them get on their feet financially. They then have opportunity to adjust to each other before the wife is faced with pregnancy and its accompaniments. However, if the commencement of the family is delayed too long it becomes more difficult to get it started. Very often in later years there are feelings of remorse and regret that the family was not commenced earlier. One of the causes of unhappiness in marriage is voluntary childlessness. With the advent of a baby into the home a new love experience is opened up. In the nurturing of little lives and the making of the sacrifices necessary to enable them to come, in turn, to maturity, some of the noblest aspects of love are realized.

A baby in the family is, of course, no sure guarantee of happiness. Sometimes the mother, preoccupied with the child, neglects her husband, and relationships worsen. A cartoon showed a baby in his diaper sitting and looking around, stating, "I'm tired of being the only thing that keeps our family together." He will not necessarily do this. However, a baby will provide a new focus for the developing love life, and when he in turn becomes a father, the grandparents will focus their love and affection on his son.

The Ultimate Challenge of Love

The process of the development of love is a gradual expansion from self to others. Climbing the road of the loving heart may sometimes be as difficult as the ascent of a mountain peak. In his poem "Excelsior," Longfellow paints the heroic picture,

> The shades of night were falling fast,
> As through an Alpine village passed
> A youth, who bore, 'mid snow and ice,
> A banner with the strange device,
> Excelsior!

Like this youth who had to turn from the inviting home, the beckoning maiden, and the warning voices in order to make his epic climb, so the traveler on the road of the loving heart is confronted with many bypasses into which he can easily turn. The climb brings its rewards and the breathtaking vista of the peak amply repays the toils of the trail. The panorama is symbolic of the progress from mere self-love to that mature love which goes out to completely exteriorized objects.

The mountain peak experience of love is the love of God. The Greek word *agape,* used to describe God's love, is said by Trench to be the word born in the bosom of revealed religion. It is nowhere used by pagan writers.

The Bible lays a heavy emphasis on love. Moses commanded his people, "Thou shalt love the Lord thy God with all thine heart, and with all thy soul, and with all thy might" (Deut. 6:5). Significantly enough the Hebrew word for love was most frequently used to describe human or family love. It is used in the moving drama of the husband-wife relationship of Hosea and Gomer. Their domestic tragedy became a prophetic parable, portraying the love of God. The long-suffering husband, following his wicked, erring, and unfaithful wife, depicts the concern of God for his people.

Jesus reminded his listeners that all the law and the prophets hung on loving God and one's fellowman. His definitive statement was, "A new commandment I give unto you, That ye love one another; as I have loved you" (John 13:34). What was new about this? There was a constant reference to loving in the Old Testament. The new feature was a new standard, "As I have loved you." He demonstrated love in action.

People do not just naturally love their fellowman. Love for others is a reflex action. God is love and a response to a divine love leads to a new attitude to our fellows. "We know that we have passed from death unto life, because we love the brethren" (1 John 3:14). The love we manifest toward others is an index of the experience of the divine encounter.

A new concern comes upon the believer's heart when he realizes his solidarity with mankind. John Donne said it beautifully:

No man is an island, entire of itself; every man is a piece of the continent, a part of the main; if a clod be washed away by the sea, Europe is the less, as well as if a promontory were, as well as if a manor of thy friends or of thine own were; any man's death diminishes me, because I am involved in mankind; and therefore, never send to know for whom the bell tolls; it tolls for thee.

It is only when a man has had an encounter with God through Christ and experienced the love of God in his own life that he really learns to love.

4
Sex—
Sinful or Sacred?

But from the beginning of the creation God made them male and female. For this cause shall a man leave his father and mother, and cleave to his wife; and they shall be one flesh: so then they are no more twain, but one flesh. What therefore God hath joined together, let not man put asunder (Mark 10:6-9).

It is a strange Old Testament command that says, "Thou shalt not seethe a kid in his mother's milk" (Ex. 23:19; 34:26; Deut. 14:21). But it is repeated three times over, twice in the book of Exodus, and once in the book of Deuteronomy, and so seems to have some special import. The restriction probably refers to the Arabian practice of preparing a gourmet's repast by cooking a kid in its mother's milk.

Other prohibitions in the Old Testament encourage an attitude of gentleness toward animals. For example, "Whether it be cow or ewe, ye shall not kill it and her young both in one day" (Lev. 22:28), or "Thou shalt not muzzle the ox when he treadeth out the corn" (Deut. 25:4). It is difficult to see why these commandments should be enjoined except for a sensitivity to the fitness of things. The Bible anticipated many of the finer feelings of groups dedicated to kindness to animals.

Our deeper sensitivities are certainly revolted by the

thought of boiling a newly slain kid in its mother's milk. It may be there was some dietary reason why it should not be done, but there is obviously a principle involved. The principle is that the milk meant to be the means of life for the newborn animal was not to be used as an instrument of destruction.

There are many applications of the principle, but one obvious area is that of the role of sex in human personality. Sex is the peculiar creative power resident within humans and the means by which life is ministered. Unfortunately, sex is all too frequently the force that deals man his most agonizing blows and after all its glowing promises leaves him in misery and suffering. Sex is associated with some of the most beautiful words in the English language—mother, home, babies, love. Yet it is often debased and linked with terms such as rape, abortion, venereal disease, and lust.

The problems arise, in part, from the complexity of the sex drive in humans. In the lower forms of animal life, sex is an instinctive, almost mechanical, urge, driving it to mating activity. But with man the same drive is surrounded by a wealth of emotions, intricately interrelated and easily thrown out of gear.

Martin Luther puzzled over the complexity of sex: "Had God consulted me in the matter, I should have advised him to continue the generation of the species by fashioning the human beings out of clay as Adam was made." Many another human must have had similar thoughts while pondering over the intricacies of the sex drive.

The wise Creator ordained that man should co-operate with him in his creative activity, and in this religion and sex are closely related. Without going as far as the fanciful interpretations of those who see all religion as the expression of the sex drive, we cannot avoid the evidences of association of sex and religion.

Some authorities think the word sex itself came originally from "six," being associated with the Sixth Commandment in the Roman Catholic version of the Decalogue, "Thou shalt not commit adultery." The Bible opens with the drama of a man-woman relationship, and through its pages are sprinkled the stories of encounters of the sexes. Standards for sexual morality come from religious sources. The idea of marriage and its degree of permanence is a distinctly Christian idea, and the mutual obligations of parents and children come primarily from religious convictions.

If religion and sex are so inextricably linked, the church must declare itself on the issues of sexual relationships. Jesus spoke out very frequently on the subject as he declared himself in the words of our text. Let us consider masculinity and femininity, sex and love, and the implications of the expression "one flesh."

Masculinity and Femininity

A professional marriage counselor doesn't generally do much preaching. However, one speculated that if ever called upon to preach he would take the text, "male and female created he them," for the essential masculinity and femininity of individuals is the raw material out of which a successful marriage relationship is built.

Although the plain facts of masculinity and femininity seem obvious, the more subtle implications frequently have been overlooked, and men are the chief offenders.

Recent writers on femininity have noted that in earlier writings the "masculine authorities" often projected their own masculinity into the situation, explaining feminine sexual reactions as essentially the same as those of the male, whereas in reality they are frequently otherwise.

But women are not blameless in the process of blunting the perception of masculinity and femininity. Women have had a long and difficult struggle to gain status recognition. It was not until 1920 that the Nineteenth Amendment gave women the right to vote in the United States. One of the dangers inherent in an aggressive femininity is that equality will be equated with "sameness," and in gaining recognition of their status women lose their distinctive femininity. It must be constantly reiterated that men and women are different.

There is an obvious *physical* difference in the sexes with the woman's body created for the task of childbearing. Some authorities claim that men and women differ in every cell of their bodies. The structural make-up of men and women is so distinctive that an expert usually can tell by looking at bones whether they belong to a male or a female.

Although we call them the "weaker sex," in reality women are physically stronger. More males are born than females, but the infant mortality rate among male infants is higher than among females; and by the time of maturity there are equal numbers of both sexes. By middle life there are about 15 per cent more women; in the seventies, 20 per cent more; and in the nineties, 50 per cent more. One authority comments, "If we choose to emphasize our survival rates as our criterion, we could teach our children that males—not females—are the weaker sex."

Psychologically, there is a wide divergence between the sexes. Women are generally more emotional than men and far more ready to respond to the emotional elements of life than to the mere factual. As a young couple walked together on a summer evening, the crickets were chirping. At the same time there came the sound of the choir singing from a nearby church. She, entranced by the choir's music said, "Doesn't it sound beautiful?"

He, listening to the crickets, responded, "Yes, I believe they make that sound by rubbing their hind legs together."

Her interest in the music and his in the mechanical were reactions typically feminine and masculine.

By the very nature of masculine and feminine anatomy, the male is the aggressor, with the woman taking the more passive role. Consequently, the man initiates the process and the woman has to be wooed and won. Associated emotions mean much more to the wife. The rhythm of her life cycle, the fatigue she is experiencing, her vague fears and apprehensions all affect the quality of her response. After an argument the husband may actually be more ready to make love because his aggressiveness has been aroused, but not so his wife. Her emotions need to be sorted out before he is acceptable to her.

Masculine "sexual excitability" is a frequently overlooked consideration. Most husbands are more easily aroused sexually and reach the peak of their desire more rapidly than do their wives. Satisfying relationships may depend on an understanding of this difference. The Bible refers to sexual experience as a man "knowing" his wife.

It takes time to really get to know each other. It has been said that it is easier to win a battle than to make love successfully.

In a well-known song the singer poses the question, "Why can't a woman be more like a man?" The answer is that God made them the way they are. Masculinity and femininity are two enriching aspects of life. These aspects have been beautifully set out in Paul's Epistle to the Ephesians, where he says that the husband is head of the wife. But while the husband is to give leadership, he is to recognize his wife's response and love his wife as Christ loved the church. One woman put it beautifully when she said, "I don't mind my husband's being the head, when he is willing to love me as Christ loved the church."

Sex and Love

The sex drive is one of man's most powerful urges, and its management causes many anxious moments. The force of the drive has caused some proponents to argue for promiscuity, claiming the sex drive is just another "hunger." It has to be satisfied, so why restrict it? Duvall has suggested some essential differences between sex and the desire for food: [1]

The denial of sexual satisfaction will produce no direct harmful physical effects. Psychologists refer to the mental mechanism of sublimation by which primitive drives of personality are redirected into new and higher channels. Thus, denial of the sex drive and sublimation into new

---

[1] Sylvanus Milne Duvall, *Men, Women, and Morals* (New York: Association Press, 1952), pp. 95–96. The following is freely adapted.

channels might pave the way for more creative aspects of personality development.

The satisfaction of physical hungers need not have any social consequences. The sex drive has awesome social responsibilities. One authority says a virile male could father a whole village of children. The birth of children is the natural outcome of sexual relationships, so a stable social situation is essential for their growth and development. In the early days of communism's accession to power in Russia, sexual promiscuity was the order of the day and the sexual act was likened to drinking from a glass of water. The situation grew so chaotic that at last Lenin was compelled to deliver his famous statement against "drinking from a dirty cup of water." Even an atheistic society discovered unbridled sexuality was not in the best interests of a stable national life.

Sex hungers differ from other hungers in that in being satisfied outside of marriage they "feed" on other people. Illicit sexuality almost invariably involves exploitation of one personality by another. One of the most depressing aspects of prostitution is the total debasement of one personality to satisfy the sex desires of another.

The wise Creator who implanted the sex drive within men and women also provided the setting of marriage for its satisfaction. In the Corinthian Epistle, when the apostle Paul uses the phrase "one flesh," as he speaks to husbands and wives, he has an obvious reference to the sexual element in marriage. The natural result of the love of husband and wife is a desire to be as close to the love object as possible and in sexual relationships they literally become "one flesh."

This husband-wife relationship provides a family setting, which allows for at least two biological factors. Humans are not like animals which have a certain period of the year when their sexual drive is at its peak. With humans sex desire remains relatively constant the whole year round. The second biological fact is the long period of helplessness in the infancy of the human in which it needs a safe and secure environment to grow. The setting for sexual relations and the secure environment for the offspring must be provided by the stable, permanent relationship of husband and wife.

Unfortunately, we live in an age with an overemphasis on sex and consequent confusion in the use of the two words, sex and love. A sexual experience is spoken of as "making love," whereas in reality it is far otherwise. Writers as far removed from each other as Reik and Duvall have noted the following essential differences between sex and love:

Sex is basically physical and, as in masturbation, there can be a sexual response without involving another personality. Love is psychical and involves the response of two personalities. It is possible to love without any physical contact. There have been love affairs in history with little if any physical relationship.

Sex may involve only a part of the personality. But love, at its best, is the response of two personalities with mental and emotional factors of as much moment as the physical.

Sex is mainly concerned with satisfying its own desires, seeking satisfaction and release without regard for the welfare of others. Love, at its highest, is unselfish. If love conflicts with sex, as when a partner is ill, the lover may be willing to forego sexual experiences. Not only are love and sex not the same but in some instances they are the very antithesis of each other.

However, although love and sex are not necessarily the same, they can, and should, be united—like steel and concrete, to build the solid structure of a strong relationship. Sex can channel and foster love in marriage and bring husband and wife closer in a bond in which they come to realize their incompleteness as individuals and their need for each other. Reik says, "The main enjoyment in sexual intercourse is not the touch of the two skins but the unconscious exchange of two roles, the secret interplay of two emotions." [2]

> And we in bodies are together brought
> So near our souls may know each other's thought
> Without a whisper.[3]

The great debate in Christian circles is about the place of sex in marriage. Some groups maintain the primary purpose of sex is begetting children and any method of planned parenthood is wrong. But in the moral issue Elton Trueblood has shown that, with the present population explosion, there is a strong case for the morality of birth control. Moreover, a whole series of pregnancies can strain a marriage. Husband and wife should not be haunted by fear of pregnancy. Yet, every child who comes into the world has a right to be expected.

Besides begetting children, sexual relations fulfil the purpose of expressing the love which two people have for each other. Sex within marriage gives a sense of fulfilment

---

[2] Theodor Reik, *Psychology of Sex Relations* (New York: Farrar and Rinehart, Inc., 1945), p. 210.
[3] Sir Francis Kynaston, "To Cynthia, on her Embraces," *Cynthiades.*

and is one of the most pleasurable experiences known to man. In marriage a husband and wife discover the pleasure they are able to give each other.

Not all sexual experiences represent fulfilment. Husbands and wives sometimes have poor sexual adjustments. Psychologists may refer to this as impotence, frigidity, and incompatibility. However, such difficulties in sexual adjustment are not necessarily the cause of marital difficulties but may be *symptoms*. A wife may use the sexual relationship as a control device, rewarding her husband when he pleases her and punishing him when he fails to please her. Similarly, a sexually aggressive and demanding husband may be motivated by a desire to dominate his wife rather than the release of his sexual tensions.

Sex should be pre-eminently creative. A husband and wife join with God in carrying on the human race. The creation of a child gives them a partnership with deity. It is creative in another way. It provides pleasure, gives release, and helps to build a solid relationship between husband and wife.

Husband and Wife Become "One Flesh"

In biblical mathematics one plus one equals one. A man plus a woman equals "one flesh." The theme runs through the Bible. In the creation story Adam looked upon his new wife and joyously exclaimed, "This is now bone of my bones, and flesh of my flesh: she shall be called Woman, because she was taken out of Man. Therefore shall a man leave his father and his mother, and shall cleave unto his wife: and they shall be one flesh" (Gen. 2:23–24).

When Jesus was faced with a question on divorce,

he answered by referring to the creation story, "They twain shall be one flesh: so then they are no more twain, but one flesh" (Mark 10:8). He significantly added, "What therefore God hath joined together, let no man put asunder."

The apostle Paul used the expression "one flesh" to describe an illicit sexual relationship. "Know ye not that he which is joined to an harlot is one body? for two, saith he, shall be one flesh" (1 Cor. 6:16). However, he also used it to illustrate the relationship of Christ and his church. The mystery of the union of Christ and the church is like the mystery of the relationship of husband and wife who become "one flesh."

In our text Jesus highlights three distinctives of a Christian marriage.

Permanency.—"What therefore God hath joined together, let not man put asunder." The biblical grounds for divorce do not include mental cruelty and incompatibility.

The highest possible human relationship.—"For this cause shall a man leave his father and his mother, and cleave to his wife." Couples who have troubles with in-laws or undue attachment to children overlook the primacy of the husband-wife relationship.

Husband and wife become "one flesh."—"They are no more twain, but one flesh." They are united in a peculiar way. A Christian marriage is an act which joins two personalities in an indissoluble union and this is the reason why the church has always had great difficulty in accepting divorce. It is like a drastic surgical procedure of cutting up a body.

Man and wife should discover a whole new life together

in marriage. George Washington Carver, the noted Negro scientist, used to tell his students that the secret of creativity was to learn to put things together in a new way. God has put men and women together in a marriage bond; and, becoming one flesh, they discover a new experience in living.

In Taoism there is a stress upon two forces—*yin* and *yang*. Everything in the universe shows the interplay of these forces and contains their characteristics in varying degrees. The *yang* is the positive or masculine force while the *yin* is the negative or feminine force. Everything in the universe contains both forces. At one time the *yin* may be stronger and another time the *yang*. In marriage the masculine and the feminine forces constantly interrelate as a significant part of the whole.

Sir Walter Scott's *Kenilworth* tells the story of the Countess of Leicester. Her husband, a nobleman in the court of Queen Elizabeth, didn't want England's virgin queen to know about his secret marriage, so he kept his wife a prisoner in his country castle. Outside her room was a trap door supported by bolts. If the bolts were removed the trap door was held in place by springs but would immediately collapse under the tiniest weight.

The two guards, Foster and Varney, had removed the bolts, and later Foster heard the sound of horses' hooves on the pavement and the sound of whistling, as when the Earl returned to the castle.

In an instant the Countess's door was flung open. She rushed onto the trap and fell to her death.

Varney's voice came through the window, "Is the bird caught? Is the deed done?"

Foster suddenly realized it was not the Earl at all.

Varney had ridden in whistling like the Earl. The Countess rushing out to meet her beloved had perished.

Foster turned on Varney and said, "Oh, if there is a judgment in heaven, thou hast deserved it, and will meet it! Thou hast destroyed her by her best affections. It is a seething of a kid in his mother's milk."

Sex should be sacred. To pervert its use is the seething of the kid in its mother's milk.

5
Marriage—
Duet or Discord?

Defraud ye not one the other, except it be with consent (1 Cor. 7:5).

Music is an integral ingredient in wedding festivities in any part of the world, but there is some confusion as to when the musical rendition should take place. The place in the ceremony differs in varying religious traditions and geographical locations.

In Australia the main musical offering comes during the interlude known as signing the register. Immediately after the minister has declared the couple to be husband and wife, the whole wedding party retires to the pastor's study where the necessary documents are signed. While the formalities are being carried out, the special music is presented. A newspaper report of a wedding ceremony will note that during the signing of the register, the soloist sang "Because" or whatever the music happened to be.

You can imagine the adjustment I had to make when after nearly twenty years of Australian ceremonies I conducted an American wedding. Immediately after I had pronounced the bride and groom to be husband and wife, the organ blared out, and they rushed from the church as if a fire alarm had sounded.

However, despite the formalities and divergences in customs, there is one type of music which should be heard at every wedding. Paul tells husbands and wives, "Defraud ye not one the other, except it be with consent" (1 Cor. 7:5). This Greek word is *sumphonia*, which literally means "sounds made together." It has come over into the English language as "symphony." So Paul is saying, "Let your marriage be a symphony."

At one church where I spoke on this subject, an unmarried lady came up and challenged the right of Paul to tell married people how to live together, commenting that a "crusty old bachelor" like Paul should not have interfered in married life. She didn't know that there are some people who think Paul may have been married. At least one commentator speculates that when Paul spoke about his "thorn in the flesh," he was referring to his wife!

In his defense before King Agrippa, Paul recounted his opposition to the Christians and said, "I gave my voice against them" (Acts 26:10). The reference may have been to the meeting of the Sanhedrin. To be a member of that body it was necessary to be married. The writer concludes that Paul was probably married as a young man and his wife died, leaving him a widower in later life.

In any case Paul was a keen student of human nature and his counsel is timeless. This word of advice to the Corinthian Christians was a frank statement on the husband-wife relationship and the obligations which it involved. However, we will not confine ourselves to Paul's statement but will follow a case study technique by taking three places in the New Testament where the Greek word *sumphonia* is used. In each instance the speaker is Jesus, as he tells of a harvest scene, a homely metaphor, and a religious experience.

The Symphony of Marriage

Jesus told a story of a farmer at harvesttime. The vines were bending beneath the weight of a bountiful crop. As the owner of the vineyard proudly inspected his vines, he noted the grapes blushing red with ripeness. He concluded that the time had come to gather in the fruitage of the vines.

Early the next morning he made off to the market place and at six o'clock talked with the men looking for work and agreed to pay them a denarius for the day's toil. Still concerned about gathering the crop, he went out at nine o'clock and hired another contingent. As the day wore on, at twelve o'clock and three in the afternoon he paid successive visits to the market place and again hired men on the same terms. Finally, as the day was drawing to a close, at five in the afternoon, with only one hour to go, he went out again and hired a final group.

With sunset came time to pay the laborers and the steward gave each the same remuneration. The men who had toiled all day were amazed to discover that the laborers who had worked for only one hour received just as much as they did. They raised their voices in protest, claiming they were entitled to more money than those who had only worked for one hour. But the owner was very specific and reminded them of their agreement to work for a denarius.

Jesus said this was a parable of the kingdom, and undoubtedly it shows a principle of service and reward. But it can also be seen as the story of human relationships in which the word "agreed" is the translation of *sumphonia*. The principle applies to the symphony of marriage, emphasizing "role" and "relationship."

The owner of the vineyard defined the respective roles of the two parties and became a little short and terse when he said, "Is it not lawful for me to do what I will with mine own?" He made it perfectly clear that his was the role of the employer and theirs the employees.

Roles in marriage is a concept which is helping us to understand more clearly what happens in the interplay of the personalities of a man and his spouse. Each individual has an image of himself and unfortunately this is often quite different from what he actually is. A second image each has is the way in which other people see him. The third image is what one really is. Altogether it might be said that there are six roles involved in a marriage relationship. The husband and wife as each really is, the two people they see themselves as being, the wife as seen by the husband, and the husband as seen by the wife. The situation might be diagramed: [1]

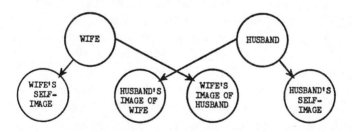

With these different views of their partners and their roles, it is small wonder that difficulties arise. One of the most unfortunate tendencies in married couples is for each to try to remake his or her spouse. The process is doomed

---

[1] Adapted from Charles W. Stewart, *The Minister as Marriage Counselor* (New York: Abingdon Press, 1961), p. 96

to failure. Each must finally accept the partner as he or she really is.

Moreover, any successful adult must continue to grow emotionally. One of the manifestations of a growth process is that the person gradually drops his defenses and comes to see himself as he really is. One measure of his maturity is how closely his self-image correlates with what he actually is.

A second concept is of relationship. The workers in the vineyard and the householder "agreed" on the terms of employment. A relationship came to exist between them. The art of relationship stands at the heart of living and this is pre-eminently true of marriage. The husband-wife relationship is the highest of all human relationships. Jesus said, "For this cause shall a man leave his father and mother, and cleave to his wife."

Other relationships are superseded. A man leaves his father and mother, and if he really can leave them the big problem of in-law difficulties is avoided. In turn the married couple's children grow and develop and as they reach the age of maturity they leave home. Wise parents learn to let their children become independent personalities. But husband and wife are still joined together. Their relationship remains and endures. "What therefore God hath joined together, let no man put asunder."

"Role" and "relationship" are words which describe two of the most important materials out of which a marriage is built. If married couples will learn to realistically know and understand themselves and their partners, and cultivate and develop the fine art of relating to a spouse in the supreme human relationship, marriage will indeed become a symphony.

The Discords of Matrimony

Jesus moves from the harvest to the home and tells about the problems besetting the housewife as she patches a worn garment. Looking around for scraps, she knows that if she patches an old garment with new material, after the first washing it will probably shrink and tear the garment (cf. Luke 5:36). The Greek word *sumphonia* which Paul used for the marriage relationship is used to describe this patching operation. The difficulty is, said Jesus, that the new material "agreeth not" with the old. It is not a symphony.

Although the ideal of married life is a symphony, it is unfortunate that the duet easily becomes a duel, the harmony discord, and the symphony a cacophony of sounds. Despite all the novelist's fantasies of romance in which it is said, "They lived happily ever after," with the implication that they entered into an unchanging relationship, there is a flux of love. In the early days of marriage two people become closely involved and bare themselves to each other. Later they discover they cannot live all their days in the highly romanticized atmosphere of newlyweds. Life cannot be a perpetual honeymoon, so ego protection becomes a factor as they develop their individual reserves.

Like the new material that "agreeth not" with the old, so disagreements come into marriages along the way. I once visited in the home of a very wealthy but somewhat belligerent man who had a subdued and retiring wife. Discussing my sermon, he challenged the statement that most couples have difficulties somewhere along the way. Turning to his wife he menacingly said, "We never have quarrels do we, Honey?" She demurely nodded her head in agreement. Obviously their completely unruffled existence was easily explicable in terms of his complete dominance of the situation.

However, in most normal husband and wife relationships, with the modern idea of a fifty-fifty marriage, both have a large part to play in the development of a good relationship. Conflict is a normal part of living. Differences will come and so a strategy must be developed to handle the situation.

Emotional reactions overshadow husband-wife relationships that are more important than intellectual misunderstandings. A marriage counselor says, "A woman may say, 'I hate my husband,' and by the very intensity with which she says it show that she loves him very much." Listen to a husband-wife quarrel and it will be seen that there is a minimum of intellectual content to their discussion. It is generally conducted on an emotional level. In the handling of emotions they can be dated, displaced, or drained.

Dated emotions are the emotional reactions which serve us well at an early stage of emotional development but are totally inadequate for an adult situation.

Bill Jones comes home from work and feels he wants to be left alone. Mary, his wife, has been in the house all day and is just as curious as a cat about what happened at work. As she bombards him with questions, Bill's irritation level rises and he lashes out and demands to know why she doesn't leave him alone and give him some peace. Mary is hurt. A difficult situation follows.

Despondent and discouraged, Bill arranges to talk with his pastor and says, "I don't know why I get so irritable with Mary. I really love her and the moment I react I could bite out my tongue. You know it is a strange thing, that's the way I used to be with my mother. She was always wanting to know where I'd been and whom I'd been out with, and I resented her interference."

To the onlooker it is all perfectly obvious. Bill is reacting with Mary in the same way he reacted to his mother. He has slipped back into his old pattern. Seward Hiltner says dated emotions can be just as unsatisfactory as dated coffee. However, stale coffee will seldom wreck a marriage but dated emotions might.

Displaced emotions also bring problems. Feeling engendered by one situation may be displaced into another. A businessman rushing to work is stopped by a policeman, who makes a sarcastic remark while making out the traffic ticket. Outwardly calm but inwardly seething, he arrives at work where his assistant reports a mistake. His superior pours out his indignation. The assistant, in turn, is short with his secretary. She goes out and finds fault with the receptionist, who then is mean to the calling salesman. He in turn goes home to criticize his unsuspecting wife. Of course it is not only husbands. The distraught wife, frustrated with the demands of the children, salesmen, and telephone canvassers may find the newly arrived husband a ready target for her hostility. It takes a pretty mature person to be able to stand off and see that his emotions have been displaced from one situation to another.

Wise husbands and wives try to avoid the difficulties of displaced emotions. One husband, after a difficult day at the office, calls up his wife and says, "Treat me kindly tonight, Honey, I've had a rough one today." A perceptive wife had an arrangement with her husband. When he came in and saw her apron on in reverse, he was to know that she had endured a rough day and needed special attention.

Drained emotions represent the process for adequately handling emotional difficulties. The expression refers to the experience in which the human expresses himself and drains off the pent-up emotion. An individual in the grip of intense emotion has been likened to an old hose blocked off at the end. As the pressure builds up something must give, and water will spurt out at the weakest spot. But if the blockage at the end is removed, and the water is allowed to escape, the situation may be righted. Speech has been called "man's most ready safety valve." An individual who gets a chance to talk is often able to drain off his emotions.

Communication is a significant word in marriage. See the young couple walking down lover's lane. By a touch of the fingers, a flutter of the eyelids, a whispered word, volumes are communicated. After some of the fantasy of courtly love has disappeared, communication often dries up. An emotional wall comes into existence. Two people may live under the same roof, eat at the same table, walk on the same carpets, and even sleep in the same bed but still be miles apart.

Rebuilding the processes of communication may be difficult. If the situation is badly deteriorated, the help of a third person may be needed. There should be no shame about going to see the minister or the marriage counselor. The aim will be the reduction of hostility so the husband and wife can have a restored communication process.

Married couples must cultivate the art of communication. There should be some time in each week when they can sit down together and discuss the affairs of the home and the status of their relationship.

When Paul said, "Defraud ye not one the other, except it be with consent," he was referring to the intimacies of married life and obviously alluded to the sexual relationship within marriage. He shows that the fine art of husband-wife relationships always involves dialogue and in all the decisions of life, even to some new commitment to God, there should be a process of communication between husband and wife.

The Master Note of Married Life

The Greek word *sumphonia* used by Paul of husband-wife relationships was used by Jesus when he said, "If two of you shall agree on earth as touching any thing that they shall ask, it shall be done for them of my Father which is in heaven" (Matt. 18:19). The picture is of a symphony of prayer with two people agreed at the mercy seat.

Married people must be agreed in many areas. They should be agreed about the budget—how they are going to spend their money. The number of children they are going to have and the way they are going to plan for their future will be vital. Whether the wife is going to work or not will be a factor in the development of their life. The question of what they will do together and what sort of mutual friends they will have must be decided. Above all of these is the important concept of a shared faith. This will give them a basis upon which to build the solid structure of their married lives together.

The novel *Lorna Doone* tells the story of Lorna,

adopted daughter of an outlaw family—the Doones. She is wooed and won by John Ridd and at last the great moment comes when they stand in the church for the wedding ceremony. John can hardly believe his good fortune as he looks at his beautiful Lorna in her lovely white wedding gown. Meanwhile, outside the church, a new act in the drama is being unfolded. Carver Doone, foster brother of Lorna, has heard of the wedding and is determined to stop it, no matter what. He comes galloping over the hill and jumps from his horse outside the church door and raising his rifle takes careful aim.

John and Lorna are pronounced man and wife and as John turns to take her into his arms and kiss her, a shot rings out. Lorna falls at John's feet with her blood staining her beautiful wedding gown.

All too often John Ridd's experience is a parable of marriage relationships. People go into marriage with such high hopes and then it seems as if it is a failure and many of the high expectations are frustrated.

But the story of Lorna Doone takes a strange turn. As John Ridd ran out to pursue Carver Doone, Lorna's friend, Ruth, took command of the situation. She refused to believe Lorna was dead and had her carried to her room, where after weeks of careful nursing Lorna was restored to health and strength again.

No marriage relationship is so badly ruptured that it may not be rebuilt. With a basic faith in Christ and his power to change life, a marriage can become a "symphony" once more.

6
Ruth,
the Daughter-in-Law

They lifted up their voice, and wept again: and Orpah kissed her mother in law; but Ruth clave unto her. And she said, Behold, thy sister in law is gone back unto her people, and unto her gods: return thou after thy sister in law. And Ruth said, Intreat me not to leave thee, or to return from following after thee: for whither thou goest, I will go; and where thou lodgest, I will lodge: thy people shall be my people, and thy God my God (Ruth 1:14–16).

The book of Judges in the Old Testament is an account of rough and rugged days. In the reading of its wars, conflicts, and turbulence it seems there was nothing but turmoil. Its pages are filled with the clash of arms and murderous plots. One scholar has suggested that the definitive statement is, "Every man did what was right in his own eyes."

Even the women seemed to have an Amazonian element to their make-up. Deborah exhorts her men and dares them to ride into battle with her. Jael, the wife of Heber, lures Sisera into her tent, sedates him with warm milk, and while he sleeps drives a tent peg into his head. Abimelech is stopped in his triumphant military adventure and meets his doom as a woman atop a tower hurls down a millstone to smash his skull.

Strangely enough, the book of Ruth comes from about

the same period of time and shows us another side of life in that far-off day. It is a pastoral scene and depicts how, that in the midst of battles and conflicts and disorders, there is always a gentler side of life in which men love, work, weep, and laugh.

In many ways the book of Ruth is a strange story. It tells of Naomi, her husband, and sons' departure from Judah to the Gentile country of Moab to escape the scourge of famine. Tragedy dogged Naomi's footsteps: first her husband's death; then her two boys, Mahlon and Chilion, departed from the tenets of their religion and married Gentile girls. Following the sons' death, the distraught mother turned her face toward Jerusalem. Her dutiful daughters-in-law gathered their meager possessions and left with her.

The moment of drama came as they stood on the border of Judah. Naomi, with nothing to offer her daughters-in-law save sorrow and disappointment, turned to them and bade them return to their own land. Orpah saw the sense of it, but Ruth refused to go. Her immortal statement has retained its poignant message through the years: "Intreat me not to leave thee, or to return from following after thee: for whither thou goest, I will go; and where thou lodgest, I will lodge: thy people shall be my people, and thy God my God" (Ruth 1:16).

Ruth, the Woman

Although ruggedly independent and willing to go into the fields and work, there was nothing masculine about Ruth. She was, in fact, as Maclaren says, an example of "the heroism of gentleness." In her gentleness is to be seen a special distinctive and unique contribution that woman can make to the world.

It has been said that old men plan wars and young men fight them. To this might be added that women stand by to worry, weep, and work.

Man has always been on the horns of a dilemma in thinking about women. In the Middle Ages, when the concept of courtly love became so prominent, as troubadours wandered across Europe singing their strange love songs, medieval man had ambivalent thoughts about women. Woman was the descendant of Mother Eve, who first tempted man. She still had a strange attraction for him and was often the means of his downfall; consequently, he felt resentful toward her. But she was also of the same sex as the virgin Mary and there were elements about her which reminded him of his own mother. In his ambivalence he was at the same time attracted to and repelled by the female figure. Elements of this ambivalence are to be seen to this very day in some of the strange fantasies of romantic love.

One of the earliest efforts to blame woman for the troubles of life is to be found in the Greek myth about Pandora's box or jar. The beautiful Pandora was given a box and told it must never be opened. Inevitably curiosity overwhelmed her and the jar top was removed. Immediately out came the demons that were to bedevil man through the years: old age, disease, insanity, oppression, envy, spite, revenge, cruelty, and every other plague that brings trouble. Fortunately, however, there was one little sprite left whose name was Hope. He popped out and gave man the ability to withstand all the others.

Is this myth telling us that while men are hard at work blaming women for their troubles, in reality it is the women who bring something extra to life? The twofold aspect of femininity is portrayed in the book of Ruth. "They said, 'Is this Naomi?'" (1:19). Sharp tongues, critical and censorious, showed one aspect of femininity. But the harsher aspects of femininity are overshadowed by the beautiful picture of the gentle Ruth in action.

The element of gentleness is always significant in life's experiences. Some years ago, in his farewell address a famous preacher said that he had pondered upon women. He was sure of their tremendous ability, yet he was amazed that they had accomplished so little in the world of affairs. They had not become great industrialists or political figures. But—after thinking it over, he had concluded that the reason for their failure was no woman ever had a *wife*.

An investigator tried to estimate the value of a wife. After considering all that she had to do—her responsibilities in the home and looking after the children—he concluded that a wife was worth about fifty-eight hundred dollars a year to her husband. The biblical writer had a higher estimate: "Who can find a virtuous woman? for her price is far above rubies" (Prov. 31:10).

A parallel to the place of Ruth in the days of judges is seen in the expansion of the franchise in the United States. The first state to grant voting rights to women was the state of Wyoming. Despite the generally accepted image of cowboys, gambling, gunmen, and cattle stampeding, it was in the city of Laramie, in 1870, that Louisa Ann Swain became the first American woman ever to cast a vote in an election. Some twenty years later, when Congress threatened to bar Wyoming's admission to the Union on the basis that women voted there, the state replied "We may stay out of the Union a hundred years, but we will come in with our women." Rough rangers of the frontier knew the value of the gentle womenfolk.

One writer has spoken about "the desensitization of twentieth-century man." A space age cannot spend all its time preoccupied with technology. Automation which sees man as less important than a punch card or a tape has left the finer sensitivities untouched. We need modern Ruths, with their all-pervading spirit of gentleness, to touch our highly refined technology.

Ruth, the Daughter-in-Law

Another unusual aspect of the book of Ruth is that it is a story, which tells of a woman's relationship to her mother-in-law. Of course, mothers-in-law are mentioned in other ancient literature, but this is one of the very few books that personifies the mother-in-law in such a favorable light. The relationship between Ruth and Naomi in many ways constitutes a model for any daughter-mother-in-law relationship.

Investigations carried on some years ago in a large American city indicated that if a marriage broke up the first twelve months it was probably because of in-law interference, and the interfering one was generally the boy's mother.

When a baby is born he is separated from his mother's body and the umbilical cord is severed. But there is an emotional umbilical cord which is much more difficult to handle. Edward A. Strecker's celebrated book *Their Mothers' Sons* tells the story of the great number of American boys who could not leave their mothers and adjust to service life. Strecker calls these mothers "moms" and says that they failed to wean their offspring emotionally.

The stereotyped mother-in-law is a fire-eating monster to be avoided at any cost. One of the stories which never fails to get a response is that of two men sitting in church. During the week they had both received a hundred dollar return on their income tax. One man decided that he would put ten dollars, the tithe of it, in the offering. The other was more close-fisted and decided not to give anything. The next day the man who gave the tithe received a telegram to tell him that he had inherited a thousand dollars. The tightfisted one also received a telegram which brought the news that his mother-in-law was coming to stay with him.

Evelyn Duvall claims that there are some old wives' tales about mothers-in-law that are wrong. She has made six specific corrective statements: [1]

1. Mother-in-law is *not* always a curse; oftentimes she is a real blessing.

2. People do *not* always find it impossible to live with or near their in-laws; many do so and like it.

3. Men are *not* more frequently annoyed by their in-laws than are women; quite the contrary.

4. Parents-in-law are *not* more critical of their children's spouses than the other way around; it is the younger generation that is the more critical.

5. Keeping quiet about in-law problems is *not* the only way to deal with them; many people prefer clearing up their differences as they arise.

---

[1] *In-laws: Pro and Con* (New York: Association Press, 1954), p. 313.

6. A person need *not* feel helpless about his in-law relationships; there is a great deal that can be done to make them satisfactory.

There are many people who have excellent relationships with in-laws and find much to commend about them. The relationship does not have to be bad if a few facts are borne in mind. Four principles emerge:

Take a good long look at your spouse-to-be's family.— One of Duvall's marriage myths is, "I'm not marrying her family, I'm marrying her." While it is true that you are only marrying your spouse-to-be, you must not overlook the fact that you will have a fairly close relationship, either socially or psychologically, with her family all your life. It may even be that you will have them *physically* near.

Answering the question, "How can I know what my wife will be like in twenty years time?," a psychologist replied, "Take a look at her mother, for she will probably be something like that."

There will probably be a *sociological* closeness. One authority suggests that the ever-lowering marriage age means more living with parents. Even if you don't live with in-laws there will be a certain amount of visiting— you in their home and they in yours. You may begin married life quite independently in another part of the country, but there is always the possibility of a time when you will have to move in with them or they with you.

It is certain that they will be close *psychologically.* The interactions built up over the years will be carried over into your life. Without being psychological determinists by saying that people must be the product of their early environment, no one can deny that this environment will continue to make its influence felt right through life. Experience also shows that young people who make even a radical break with home frequently return psychologically at a later date to the experiences of their early environment.

The girl who just couldn't wait to get away from her home and family often *wants* her mother when the baby is born or her sister when some other trouble arises.

Mutual acceptance is basic.—Psychologists have taught us the importance of acceptance. It means seeing and knowing people for what they are and accepting them, without necessarily approving or disapproving of their behavior.

In the ministry of Jesus and his relationship with the woman taken in adultery we see an illustration of acceptance. She was brought to him with all the evidence of her transgression of the very standards for which he stood. His words of response, "Neither do I condemn thee" (John 8:11), are indicative of the fact that although she did not conform to what he believed was right, he accepted her as a person and was willing to offer her a chance to grow spiritually and emotionally so that she could handle life's problems.

"They [in-laws] accept me" was the response of 40.9 per cent of those participating in a survey conducted by Duvall.[2] Obviously, this is the most significant single factor in good in-law relationships.

Have respect for each other.—A good piece of advice to young couples would be that they should avoid living

---

[2] *Ibid.,* p. 375.

with their in-laws if at all possible. The circumstances of life sometimes make it necessary to unite in a joint domestic enterprise with the in-laws. When this is true, there should be a definite understanding as to the responsibilities which each has to the other. The do's and don't's should be clearly defined at the beginning, before emotion clouds the issues.

Both sides will have to work at it. The in-laws will see all the silly mistakes the newlyweds make, and there is a good chance that the newlyweds will in turn feel that the older people are fuddy-duddies. Grandparents often dote over the grandchildren, but there comes a certain time when they realize they don't want to spend their lives just being perpetual baby-sitters.

Duvall's study showed that 34.3 per cent of the respondents who felt good about their in-law relationships attributed this to a mutual respect for each other.

The channel of communication should be through the relative.—If there is trouble with the boy's mother and something needs to be said to her, then it should be the boy's responsibility to do the telling. If there is trouble with the girl's parents then the girl should be the one who conveys the information.

As in all relationships in life, communication is the key. One young couple was having trouble with her parents who came to stay with them every second weekend. A counselor recommended that they should be frank with the parents, but they did not want to offend them. Finally, because the channels of communication were not open, the couple accepted a job in a distant state. Then it was possible for her parents to visit them only once a year.

The important element of marriage is commitment. It is not a matter of a boy or a girl's ignoring the parents. Each has made a new commitment in life and has been able to see the new line of priorities. If the priority of commitment to one's spouse is kept in mind then many in-law difficulties will be overcome.

Ruth, the Woman of Faith

The words of Ruth have a peculiar significance. As she stood on the border of Moab and made the declaration that she was renouncing the gods of her people and the country of her birth, she took on an entirely new allegiance. As Ruth threw herself on Naomi's withered breast she "clave" unto her. This same Hebrew word was used in the statement that a man should cleave unto his wife. Later it was used to describe the experience of Eleazar, when his "hand clave unto the sword" (2 Sam. 23:10). He could not put the sword down. In his parting counsel to Israel, Joshua exhorted them to "cleave unto the Lord, your God."

Spurgeon's college in England has on its crest the image of a hand holding to a cross and a Latin inscription which, being interpreted, reads, "I hold and am held." Jesus said of those who put their trust in him, "I give unto them eternal life; and no man shall ever pluck them out of my hand." We can safely commit ourselves to him without any reservation and be sure that he will keep us.

Ruth was a Gentile, but as we turn to the book of Ruth and read the genealogy, we discover she was an ancestor of David and, consequently, of Jesus. Born outside the privileged race, she became part of the line of inheritance by which the Saviour came into the world. From this I

learn that whosoever I am, I need not despair. God wants
me in his family. Faced with the Father God who loved
me and gave his Son to die for me, I can say with Ruth,
"Thy people shall be my people, and thy God my God"
(1:16).

7
Facts of Life for Fathers

The king was much moved, and went up to the chamber over the gate, and wept: and as he went, thus he said, O my son Absalom, my son, my son Absalom! would God I had died for thee, O Absalom, my son, my son! (2 Sam. 18:33).

The words of our text are among the bitterest cries ever to fall from the lips of a human being. Full of pathos and concern, they might have come as an anguished wail from the heart of a devastated woman. But they came from the man, King David, representing his feelings of failure and frustration in one of the darkest moments of his colorful life.

King David was remarkable in many ways. Starting with the modest occupation of tending sheep on the hillside, he ultimately became king of his people. Blessed with unusual gifts of leadership and the capacity to issue a challenge, he was able to call forth a response from his followers, who left hearth and home to join his band of freebooters. Living in the mountains under the contagion of his personal magnetism, David's mighty men wrote a new and illustrous page in Israel's history.

Listening to the song of the bird, the rustling wind, and the babbling brook, the shepherd boy took his harp and strummed the songs until he became known as "the sweet singer of Israel." The book of Psalms contains many of his songs that stir the whole gamut of emotions—from the depth of despair in Psalm 31 to the serene confidence of Psalm 23.

Referred to as a man after God's own heart, David had clear, spiritual perception. Human and earthy, at his worst a great sinner, at his best he was a great saint. The spiritual precepts from his pen have been a source of inspiration through the centuries.

A remarkable statesman, David took a poor, dispirited little kingdom and by his direction molded the heterogeneous elements into a compact and unified nation. The prosperity attended upon his reign reached such a high level that his era is often referred to as "the golden age of Israel."

However, while David was successful as a leader, poet, singer, king, and man of spiritual insight, the words of our text remind us that he was a failure as a father. It is appropriate, then, to consider David's experience in an effort to discover how important a father's influence is in personality development.

The Importance of a Father Figure

In the days of David there was no doubt as to the role of the father in the home. The man was in full and complete control. Some of the experiences recorded in David's life are a sad commentary on the status of women in that day, when men had the all-important position in society. In modern times a somewhat different situation has developed. Some observers have characterized it as "the effeminization of American society." Sociologists have speculated that while the men were out on the frontier endeavoring to tame the wilderness and carve out a new empire, it was inevitable that women should be left at home to care for the family and accept responsibility for local politics.

A favorite story on one air force base is that of an attentive Japanese wife who waited hand and foot upon her American husband. She shocked the American wives by her devotion to him. On the day that she received United States citizenship her husband sank into his easy chair and as usual called for his slippers. To his amazement, she replied, "I'm an American citizen now. Get them yourself!"

Vance Packard in his book *The Status Seekers* shows the place which women occupy in different cultures. In many foreign cultures there is no doubt that the husband is in charge of the household. Among the lower classes within our own culture, the father often gives strict supervision to the activities of the family. In the large middle class, which comprises a very important section of American culture, wives tend to be in charge of the family affairs. The husbands are not nearly so important. The father goes out to earn the living and is often away from early morning until late at night, so responsibility for the family falls upon the mother. She is the chauffeur, the disciplinarian, the arbitrator in fights and discussions, the housekeeper, and the bill-payer.

A man growing up in our American culture may spend all of his days under the care of a woman. He has a woman for a mother. As soon as he is old enough, it may be that she will go off to work and leave him under the care of another woman who is his baby-sitter. At school he discovers one of the tragedies of our American educational system—that a great portion of the teachers are women. So a growing schoolboy may remain constantly under the supervision of a woman. The youngster at last finishes high school. It could be that he might be exposed to a masculine figure in college, but he then looks around for some woman whom he can marry so that she will be able to watch over him, care for him, perhaps even put him through college, and then share the rest of his days with him. Thus, the overshadowing female may be a constant support to the frail male through all the days of his earthly pilgrimage.

Growing boys need a masculine figure in their lives. Louis P. Thorpe has given an excellent summary of what a father means to a boy. The father represents *the man* the boy will grow to be as he accepts his *masculine role in life*. He symbolizes in many ways the *workaday world* which is outside the home; he is the symbol of the *authority* with which the boy must identify; he represents the husband-lover that the boy will someday be and the *father-parent* he will become. A boy needs a father, not just an "assistant mother." As Margaret Mead has put it, the father should be more than the "children's mother's husband."

Social science investigators have been calling attention to the importance of the masculine figure in a developing boy's life. The Korean War jolted American complacency with the news that for the first time in American history twenty-one G.I.s had elected to stay in enemy hands. Virginia Paisley investigated their background and found that out of the twenty-one, nineteen of them felt unwanted by their fathers or stepfathers. She further discovered that eleven of the twenty-one lost their fathers at an early age, either by divorce or by death. Obviously, these boys had personality defects which came, in part at least, from lack of an adequate father figure in their lives.

Similarly, with women there are indications of the necessity for a strong masculine figure in their lives. Thorpe tells us that to a girl a father is important. He represents the symbol of what men are like (masculinity). He is the representative *head of the family*—breadwinner and economic provider. He is the *symbol of authority*, to which she must submit or follow. He is the *father-parent* with whom she will one day share her motherhood and the *lover-husband* she will someday have.

In a recent issue of a magazine an article entitled "The Search for a Phantom Father" discussed the tragedy of office romances of girls in the twenty-five or thirty-five-year-age bracket who became involved with males many years their senior. The men never intended to desert their wives and from the girls' viewpoint the future of such a romance was very bleak. Nevertheless, some girls risked everything for their romantic fling. From his investigations the writer concluded that one reason for the romances was an unsatisfactory father figure. The girls' fathers had often been a "Mr. Milquetoast" or were in some other way unsatisfactory. Now, they were really searching for a father. It was indeed "the search for a phantom father."

A recent newspaper item told of four youths and a girl in a great American city who had robbed and tortured a man. In the terrible story it was revealed that the girl had used a pair of scissors to carve eight-inch letters on the man's back. Seeking to give an explanation for her behavior she said, "Because I hate my father and he looks like him." One wonders what sort of story could be told about the father figure in this girl's life.

Sociologists have also been pointing out the importance of father figures. Sheldon and Eleanor Glueck, in their book *Predicting Delinquency and Crime,* have set up a fivefold criteria with which it is possible to predict with considerable accuracy the future criminal career or experience the delinquency of a child. Of the five factors involved in predicting what was going to happen in the lives of children, two have to do with the father—his discipline and his relationship with his son.

In an investigation carried out at a large seminary with leaders in religious education, an effort was made to discover how important father figures were in the lives of these people. It was discovered that successful leaders had almost invariably come from homes where there were good father figures. Unsuccessful leaders had just as invariably been associated with homes where there were unsatisfactory father figures.

Far more important than all of the foregoing is the discovery by psychologists that there is a tendency for the child to *make God in its father's image.* In a Christian counseling center it was found that in many cases of problems concerning religious faith there was some type of parental difficulty in the background with the father more significant than the mother. If the father was cruel and repressive, God was feared and resented. In cases where the father was casual and negligent, the child tended to be indifferent to God. Where the father was inconsistent in his discipline, the individual found it difficult to ever trust God.

All of this is saying that whether we look at it psychologically, sociologically, or from the purely religious point of view, the father is of vital importance in the developing life of the child.

The Father Who Failed

The words of the text tell of a father who failed. Because so many fathers fail, an examination of this father's failure may reveal pitfalls to be avoided.

David missed his opportunity with his son Absalom. In most areas of life it is possible to make a mistake and later on return to try again. But in an experience of rearing children it is not possible to go back and start over again. A child cannot go back and become a child. He must, of necessity, continue to grow. Psychologists speak of the "teachable moment." There is a certain moment in experience when an individual is ready to learn a lesson. If he does not learn the lesson at this particular time, in all probability he will never learn it at all and future development may be unsatisfactory. Shakespeare said it in *Julius Caesar*:

> There is a tide in the affairs of men,
> Which, taken at the flood, leads on to fortune;
> Omitted, all the voyage of their life
> Is bound in shallows and in miseries.

If a father's role is not fulfilled at the appropriate time in the developing child's life, his great opportunity will have been missed. As Esau found no place for repentance, so with us; there may be no chance to go back and undo the past.

David shifted the responsibility for looking after his son. As he dealt with his son he gave the task of relaying messages to other people, using intermediaries and expecting them to accept responsibility for looking after him. In the last tragic episode of his experience he requested the officers going off to war to "deal gently with the young man." Naturally, these men made an independent judgment and when they came upon Absalom, hanging from a tree by his raven locks, thrust in the vengeful spear. Someone has said that Absalom never went to his father with a broken toy; consequently, he never went to him with a broken heart.

In the area of religion an experiment carried out in a seminary discovered that in the experience of religious awakening there were four influential figures—the mother, the minister, the father, and the Sunday school teacher. It is a sad commentary upon the influence of a father that he should have had less influence in the spiritual experience of his child than did the minister. The time has come when the responsibility for the character development of the children must be fairly and squarely laid at the feet of each father.

David was busy about many important things—leading a people, ruling a nation, writing beautiful poetry. Was this busyness really a cover-up? Speaking in another connection, a writer has said that busyness is one of the most acceptable escape mechanisms of our day. The important thing is not how much we are doing but with what we are occupied. There are so many men who are busy making a living, piling up money and assets, and forgetting the all-important task of rearing sons and daughters. To paraphrase a challenging Scripture verse, "What shall it profit a man, if he gain the whole world, and lose his own son or daughter?"

David set a bad example. He became a prodigal in the darkest moment of his life and murdered a man in an effort to cover his misdemeanor. Later, he became a great saint. God forgave him and welcomed him back. David came to be spoken of by the inspired writer as a man after God's own heart. Gifted with spiritual insight, through his writings he ministered to the generations yet to be, but his saintly living never brought Absalom, who had followed him into the far country, back into contact with God. Although David came back, Absalom didn't bother to come with him. The example a father leaves before his child will always be one of the most telling and vital things that he ever does.

The Enrichment of the Fatherhood Concept

Right through the Old Testament there is a constant concern for the "fatherless" and there are many exhortations to the Jewish people to accept responsibility for caring for those left without fathers. Experiments by psychologists have shown that substitute parents are often very good. It is not the biological fact of fatherhood but the emotional relationship that comes to exist. Since many fathers will not accept the responsibility for their children, Christian men often have to step out and become substitute fathers, as they work with boys in the organizational life of the church.

Unfortunately, many men do not think about their responsibility of being adequate fathers. I once addressed a Dads' Club in an influential area of the city. After the meeting was over one of the officers thanked me for the talk and said that in all his years of attending the Dads'

Club this was the first time anyone had ever spoken on the importance of being a good father.

In biblical times great responsibility was placed on the fathers' shoulders, but we have all too easily shrugged it off. Many marriage counselors feel that women are much more ready than men are to study child psychology. We must take time to learn the art of fatherhood, just as we do to learn any other skill.

Some of David's greatest writings came from his bitterest experiences. It might well be that Psalm 103, traditionally described as "a psalm of David" sprung from his spiritual insights at the news of Absalom's death. One of David's most definitive writings about the nature of God, this psalm contrasts the frailties of man with the grandeur and greatness of God. Despite the magnitude of God, David asserts and reasserts his patience and mercy in the glad assurance that "as far as the east is from the west, so far hath he removed our transgressions from us." In the central verse of the psalm he states his over-all theme, "Like as a father pitieth his children, so the Lord pitieth them that fear him" (v. 13).

In the Bible the term "Father" is a favored one for describing God. The most graphic story Jesus ever told was of the son's going into the far country and of the father's waiting for him to come back home again. Jesus frequently reminded his followers of the relationship between God and his children. He told them that God would watch over them far more carefully than any earthly father would. In the great pattern for prayer life set out by Jesus, he taught men to say, "Our Father which art in heaven." Here we see the idealized fatherhood, which represents fatherhood at its highest, in the wonder of the love of God for men and women.

This Father who is in heaven wants a relationship with his children, and such a relationship can only come when an individual has an experience of faith in Christ and, consequently, becomes a child of God. The relationship is made possible by the death of Christ upon the cross. Through this, God invites people to have the experience of the new birth and become children of the living God.

"Bleak House," one of Charles Dickens' most moving stories tells of Jo, the crossing sweeper. Jo works at his humble task, sweeping the crossing and hoping for the pennies which people will throw to him. On one occasion he is asked about his father and mother. His response is, "I neber knowed nothing about 'em." Later in the story Jo is ill, lying in a dismal attic room. He is attended by a kind Christian doctor, Allan Woodcourt.

The doctor speaks to the sinking boy and asks, "Do you hear me, Jo?"

Jo responds, "I hear you, Sir. It's dark, but I'm a-groping, I'm a-groping. Let me catch hold of your hand."

Dr. Woodcourt says, "Can you say what I say?"

Jo responds, "I'll say anything you say, for I know it is good."

The doctor says, "Our Father which art in heaven."

Jo replies, "Yes, that's wery good, Sir, wery good," and with that, Jo, who "neber knowed nothing" about his father or mother entered into the most wonderful of all relationships as he passed into the presence of his Heavenly Father.

As vital as fatherhood is and as significant as the father figure is in the life of the growing individual in the family unit, it is important that fathers be at their best. No man can ever be at his best without a right relationship with God. Above everything else, he who is to be an adequate father must have God as his Father.

8
The Family Meal

He was known of them in breaking of bread (Luke 24:35).

Whenever I speak to a group on the subject of meals and am conscious of my accent, I recall the following story.

During World War II, at a banquet given in Washington, a young inexperienced American diplomat found himself sitting next to Wellington Koo, the Chinese ambassador. The young diplomat, feeling he should do something in the interest of international relations, tried to strike up a conversation. During the first course he asked, "Likee soupee?" Dr. Koo nodded his head to show he was enjoying the soup. Later the chairman called Dr. Koo to the platform to address the gathering. Dr. Koo spoke to them in faultless, impeccable English. When he returned to his seat, he turned to his now somewhat crestfallen young friend, and asked, "Likee speechee?"

It was my privilege some years ago to spend a week on Herron Island. A tremendous coral palisade stretching some thirteen hundred miles down the northeastern coast of Australia, Herron Island is part of the Great Barrier Reef. Two friends and I spent the week photographing the wonders of nature. Among my pictures is one of a bird sitting on the limb of a tree.

There is a time of the year when the noddy tern's heart lightly turns to love. Flying back from a day's fishing, he has his eyes wide open for some female noddy tern with whom he can make a match. When at last he sees a prospect, he flutters down on the branch of the tree near his female counterpart. He begins to make strange noises and to move closer. As his test progresses, he regurgitates a fish. If his friend avidly seizes the fish, then all is well; they are going steady, and another noddy tern home is in prospect. If, on the other hand, she refuses the proffered morsel, he once again pursues his search. With certain necessary refinements, this is the story of love the wide world over.

One outstanding psychiatrist has told us that the first natural impulse is to try to feed a loved one. If eating occupies such an important part in the development of love life, it will naturally follow that mealtime experiences will have special significance not only during courting days but right through family life.

Although the Bible is a book of spiritual truth, it has much to say about material things. The processes of a meal may seem mundane and ordinary, but the Bible gives much space to mealtime experiences and the lessons to be learned from them. The records may represent a sensory approach to the teaching, for almost invariably when the mealtime experiences are recounted, there is some special teaching involved.

The justice of God was seen at the feast of Belshazzar. This meal was prepared for a thousand lords, and in the midst of all the drunkenness and revelry, there came a dramatic moment. A hand wrote on the wall that Belshazzar had been weighed in the balance and found wanting.

The banquet table experience, at which he gave vent to his unbridled appetite, was with poetic justice the place where judgment was passed upon him.

During the wilderness wanderings of the children of Israel, they were fed with a special food called manna. The manna had to be gathered with care. Those gathering more than they needed found they had none left over and those who gathered only small amounts had sufficient. Just enough was to be gathered for each day. On the day before the sabbath, twice as much was collected so they could rest on the sabbath. However, if this much was gathered on any other day it deteriorated and had to be thrown away. It is not difficult to imagine the children excitedly picking up the manna, according to the rules. Through it all, the parents carefully explained to the children the message of God's providential care.

A whole chapter in the book of Leviticus is given to telling the Israelites what food they could or could not eat. In all probability there were certain wise dietary restrictions necessary for a nomadic people wandering through the wilderness. But from the careful descriptions given to the various types of food, it becomes obvious that the children of Israel were being reminded that they were a "peculiar" people. Being unlike other people, they had to eat a special type of food. To this very day the Jewish people have remained distinctive in their eating habits.

Possibly one of the most dramatic events in the Israelite household was the Passover supper. As the family sat around the table for the special meal, perhaps a child would ask, "What mean ye by this service?" The father would explain how God had delivered them out of Egypt.

So the child early learned that God watched over and cared for Israel.

The New Testament tells of Jesus' gathering with his disciples in the upper room for the Passover supper. As he placed his hands upon the bread and the cup of wine, he gave the symbols new meaning. From this time on they were to memorialize his broken body and shed blood. To the Christian, perhaps the most significant single event in his church life is when the church family gathers around the Lord's table to eat the bread and drink the wine, thus remembering the Lord's death till he come.

A Teaching Situation

Right through the Bible meals were associated with great religious lessons. The circumstances of the meal, the peculiar regulations, restrictions, and associations were geared to teaching great lessons about God to his people.

Some sociologists have seen a particular significance about the dining table and the teaching opportunity it affords. Even the place where a member of the family chooses to sit may show his attitude toward other members of the family or define his role in the family's life. In many homes it is the only place where the whole family is ever gathered at one time. Much family conferring, planning, and decision-making is carried on at mealtime.

In an effort to discover the nature of mealtime experiences, some investigators persuaded families to place tape recorders under their tables to record what transpired. The results revealed a strange variety of experiences.

Some families spend all their time *criticizing other people*. Apparently, they not only consume their food but "eat out" the neighbors as well. It is generally agreed that this is a poor type of mealtime experience and indicative of a family which produces antisocial and unpopular people.

Other families apparently spend most of their mealtime *quarreling*. If there is one time when it is better than another to quarrel with members of the family it is certainly not at mealtime. We do not have to have doctors to tell us that the process of digestion is not helped when one is upset emotionally.

The third type of dining experience is that which produces what someone has called the *show-offs* and *smart alecks*. The family gathered to eat provides an excellent ready-made audience.

Some years ago I visited in the home of a psychiatrist. We were old friends, having served together in an Army hospital. As we sat at breakfast, he displayed a strange detachment toward his family. He focused his total attention on me, as he explained a case he was handling, in which he thought I would be interested.

While listening to my friend, I peered out of the corner of my eye to the end of the table, where the smallest member of the family sat in a high chair. Before him was a large plate of cereal covered with milk. I mentally noted the possibilities of the situation. As my friend continued to elaborate on the case, I saw the little boy climb to his feet. He looked around for a moment, then reaching over lifted up his plate, pouring milk and cereal everywhere. At last my friend paused for a moment, looked at the little fellow, then remarked, "I wonder what he's trying to say." According to investigators, many families are trying to say things by their behavior.

The most successful type of dining table experience is

what some investigators have called the *interpretive*. The family has a sense of being together. They can discuss serious matters with appropriate humor. World events as well as the trivial matters of family life can be discussed. Or this may be an opportunity for the family council to function.

In many homes the little rituals of life are observed at the table. The family members bow their heads and ask God's blessing upon their food. Prayer is offered and often a hymn is sung and the Scriptures read. Anniversaries, birthdays, and the great patriotic holidays are celebrated. Such observances serve as a stabilizing force in family life.

However, modern times have brought a new and deadly enemy to satisfying mealtime experiences. On his adventures while searching for the Golden Fleece, Ulysses and his men had the misfortune to fall into the hands of a one-eyed monster named Cyclops. They had hoped to escape while Cyclops slept but found to their dismay that at night he stretched himself across the entrance to the cave. So the Argonauts took a large piece of lumber and burned the end of it in the fire until it was red hot. Lifting it to their shoulders, they carried it over and drove the red hot end into one eye of the giant and blinded him.

The modern Cyclops is called television—the one-eyed monster that captures many families and locks them in a dimly lit prison house. We do not have to smash the picture tube on the television, it would be too expensive. There is a convenient switch, which is easy to manage. The maturity of the family may be detected by observing what programs it watches on television.

Some years ago a Broadman film titled *Bible on the Table* told the story of a boy who tried to persuade his father to read the Bible as they sat together at mealtime. The father was lukewarm about the idea and declared himself very forthrightly, "I don't eat my breakfast in church and I don't want church with my breakfast." Nevertheless, as the story developed there came a moment when he became concerned about his daughter's values and one morning took up the Bible and began to read. A mealtime experience like this might easily transform the whole temper and spirit of a family.

Fellowship

The early church had a number of practices different to ours. One of these was the love feasts, where members of the church gathered, ate a meal, and fellowshiped together. Fellowship was of vital importance in the early church. After the day of Pentecost the disciples continued steadfastly in the apostle's doctrine—breaking of bread, prayers, and fellowship. By putting fellowship on a level with these other significant practices, the Bible indicates its vital role in Christian experience. So we, too, can symbolize and portray the Christian experience of fellowship at the meal table.

While a seminary student, I was pastor of a small church. One Wednesday, before conducting the evening service, I visited in the home of Mrs. Duncan, a godly Scotch widow. As I arrived at her home she emerged from her kitchen with perspiring brow to seat me at the table. The snowy linen cloth with the silver brought by the Scotch bride to Australia was set for one person. She explained she was too nervous to eat.

As I sat in my lonely grandeur at the table, she would rush into the kitchen to emerge with the first course, place it in front of me, sit down and fix me with an eagle eye. She had no interest in conversation and sat with never a word. As I finished each loaded plate she would spring to her feet, seize the empty plate, rush to the kitchen, and bring back still more.

So the meal progressed in dead silence. When at last the meal was finished, I read the Bible and prayed, shook hands, and departed. It was a beautiful meal, sacrificially prepared, tastefully served, but we had no fellowship. It was more as if I were the maharajah and she my devoted slave.

Contrast this with an Army experience. When we went out to the rifle range for a practice shoot, we carried what were appropriately called "iron rations," which consisted of two packages of what we called "dog biscuits" and a can of bully beef. One man carried rations for three; consequently, the other two didn't let him out of their sight. By noontime the bully beef was good and hot and greasy. The can was opened, the meat slopped out on the plate. Taking his bayonet, the officiating soldier made marks in two places on the meat. If his two comrades agreed this was a fair and equitable distribution, he sliced the meat into three pieces. Each man stabbed a piece and sat chewing on it, and when I say chewing on it, I mean chewing on it.

We were demonstrating the Christian concept of fellowship, for the Greek word *koinonia*, translated "fellowship," literally means "going shares." Classical usage describes a soldier's carrying his rations on his back and sharing them with his fellow soldiers.

The dining table can give an excellent illustration of fellowship. In our family we use the mystic initials F.H.B.

The arrival of visitors is preceded by a briefing session in which my wife tells each of us just what is expected. At the table the platter of fried chicken goes around a second time. Just as I am about to take a piece of white meat, my wife whispers, "F.H.B." so I choose a wing or a back, as if this were my preferred portion of the chicken. In our family, as in many others, F.H.B. means "Family Hold Back." Visitors come first. This is part of the process of having fellowship at the family meal.

On many occasions Jesus sat down with people for fellowship meals. He was often in the home of Mary, Martha, and Lazarus. He ate with his disciples, he shared with the five thousand, and after walking the dusty road to Emmaus with two disciples he "was known of them in breaking of bread" (Luke 24:35). The mealtime experience can be a real time of fellowship.

An Evangelistic Opportunity

A tax gatherer—wealthy, comfortable, but disillusioned —sat in his office in Capernaum. He had heard of the prophet who was proclaiming a message opposed to everything for which he had lived. Then one day a shadow fell across the entrance to his tax collector's booth. The prophet looked at him and said, "Follow me." Immediately Matthew left all and followed him.

Concerned about his fellow tax-gatherers, he was anxious that they too should meet the Saviour of mankind. So the scheming Matthew devised a way. He invited them to a meal where Jesus was the guest of honor. This is probably the first record of an effort to use a meal as an evangelistic opportunity.

An old adage says, "The way to a man's heart is through

his stomach." There is an element of truth in the statement and the church can capitalize on mealtime experiences for evangelistic purposes. Looking back over my
ministry, some of the best professions of faith in Christ
that I can recall are those who first visited in our home.
In this way we established a relationship, making it easier
for them to later profess their faith in Christ.

One fascinating aspect of all this is that a relationship
with God is sometimes spoken of under the metaphor of
eating a meal. The psalmist sounded his evangelistic invitation by saying, "O taste and see that the Lord is good"
(34:8). In the story that Jesus told about the gospel invitation he used the metaphor of a great feast, bountifully
provided. God was inviting people to come, for all things
were now ready. Despite the gracious invitation, many
turned aside and "they all with one consent began to
make excuse" (Luke 14:18).

Why do people not accept the invitation to the gospel
feast? There are many answers, but one of the most important is that they do not realize what they are missing.
When I was on the island of Morotai I was thrilled to hear
the news of the release of some Dutch missionaries, who
had been Japanese prisoners of war. I traveled across to
visit with them and found them living in a little grass hut.
We had a wonderful time. About noon I prepared to de-
part, but they insisted that I stay.

The Australian Army had strange ideas about what food
the troops should eat. Apparently, sheep tired of living
periodically gave themselves up for mincemeat. Added
to this were vegetables of uncertain age and the end result
was a concoction called M and V—meat and vegetables.

You can imagine my horror when I sat at the Bott

table to discover that the Australian Army also supplied their rations. The meal was to be "M and V." I tried to think of some way out of my difficulty. I *could* suddenly get sick and not be able to eat; or I *could* remember an appointment, which would mean getting back to camp immediately. While I mentally battled out the situation, Mrs. Bott asked her daughter Wilhelmina to ask God's blessing on the food. The little girl rattled off in Dutch, "Thank you, God, for this delicious food."

At the conclusion, I leaned over and said, "Wilhelmina, this is not delicious food."

Her mother interrupted, "It might not be delicious to you but a little girl who has lived for years in a prison camp finds it delicious."

Not having tasted the best, she was satisfied with second best. Many people who have never had a vital religious experience do not realize what Christ can mean to them. They are satisfied with second best.

The most winsome and wooing invitation in the Bible is, "Behold, I stand at the door, and knock: if any man hear my voice, and open the door, I will come in to him, and will sup with him, and he with me" (Rev. 3:20). Salvation is likened unto eating a delicious and satisfying meal.

> Come, for the feast is spread;
> Hark to the call!
> Come to the Living Bread,
> Broken for all;
> Come to His house of wine,
> Low on His breast recline,
> All that He hath is thine;
> Come, sinner, come.
>
> P. P. BLISS

9
Church and Family—
Allies or Enemies?

Rebuke not an elder, but intreat him as a father; and the younger men as brethren; the elder women as mothers; the younger as sisters, with all purity (1 Tim. 5:1–2).

The apostle Paul may not have known the bliss of family life but he certainly did have a love for individuals. He never let his preoccupation with theological concepts cause him to overlook the individual.

Paul was closer to some individuals than others. A particularly close bond existed between him and the young man Timothy. Timothy's mother and grandmother were devout believers. They may have become Christians during Paul's first missionary journey. Timothy's father was apparently a pagan. When Paul passed through the city of Lystra on the second missionary journey with Silas, he was strangely drawn to Timothy. He even invited him to join them as they continued their mission. Thus began an ever-growing relationship between Paul and Timothy.

In the closing moments of Paul's life his thoughts were of the young man. So he took his pen in hand and wrote two letters—the first and second epistles to Timothy. He tried to boost the young man's morale by warning him, "Let no man despise thy youth" (1 Tim. 4:12). Again he wrote, "Flee also youthful lusts" (2 Tim. 2:22). He sought to bring out his masculinity by challenging him to "endure hardness, as a good soldier of Jesus Christ" (2 Tim. 2:3).

Timothy needed encouragement, for his was no easy task. He was the pastor of a church, and with the early drive of missionary enterprise beginning to die, a work of consolidation and organization had to be undertaken. Problems of church organization and leadership pressed in on the youthful minister. Paul's letters, significantly enough called the pastoral epistles, laid down principles of church government and suggested plans of organization.

The home and the church are basic institutions of society. Older than the church, the family has a peculiar relationship to it. In these letters to Timothy, Paul maintains that the two basic sociological units affect each other and that there should be a strong relationship between them.

The Family Principle in Church Life

Paul sets out an unusual plan of organization for a church. He says, "Don't reprimand a senior member of your Church; appeal to him as a father. Treat the young men as brothers, and the older women as mothers. Treat the younger women as sisters, and no more" (1 Tim. 5:1–2).[1] It is the family principle of organization which is applicable to all areas of church life.

The high executive is sometimes pictured as saying to a subordinate, "We are just one big happy family around here." All too frequently the whole thing has all the earmarks of being phony. The church is not just another business organization, it has certain distinctives. It is all

---

[1] From *The New Testament in Modern English*, © J. B. Phillips, 1958. Used with permission of The Macmillan Company.

too easy for a church to develop into a business. The church members are the shareholders, the pastor the president, and the deacons the board of directors. This plan of organization is not that of the New Testament.

The New Testament sets forth the "family plan" of church administration. "The church family" is a rich expression often used to describe a given church and its members. According to Paul, the term comes close to the ideal. The common interest, the diversity of personalities, the shared concern, and the closely defined objectives of the group are all points of similarity between the family and the church organization.

The family principle obtains in *church relationships*. There is a delicate interplay of relationships within a family that Paul felt should be developed and maintained in church life: "Don't reprimand a senior member of your church, appeal to him as a father. Treat the young men as brothers, and the older women as mothers."

It is easy for the young preacher to see the shortcomings of the older members who seem unwilling to follow new ideas. He must remember, however, that they have borne the heat and burden of the day and have proved their loyalty and steadfastness over the years. The younger members of the church are sometimes frivolous and lightheaded and it is easy to write them off. So Paul points Timothy to the "growth" principle in family relations.

In the family the infant grows to be a child, the child a man, and thus roles change with passing years. The foolish schoolboy may be tomorrow's deacon and the giggling girl may in the years ahead be the missionary. Paul is reminding Timothy of the necessity of respecting older members for what life's experience has done with them and being patient with younger members, anticipating what they will become in the future.

The family principle in *interpersonal relationships* carries over into relationships with the opposite sex. What better advice could be given a young preacher than, "Treat the young women as sisters, and no more"? The pathway of the Christian enterprise is littered with men who start out with so much promise but become involved emotionally, bringing only heartache, despair, and remorse.

The family principle also applies in *leadership qualifications*. Concerned about the qualifications of leaders, Paul evaluates them in part by the quality of their family relationships. Theological education has become increasingly complex. Many theological students now study not only books but also "the living human document." The student works in an institution such as a hospital, where he receives clinical pastoral training. Learning to relate to needy people helps him develop leadership skills.

Perhaps Paul anticipated some of the insights of clinical pastoral education. The elder must be "the husband of one wife." He is to show he can enter into a lasting relationship with another person and maintain a permanent loyalty. While seeing his partner's foibles and shortcomings, he can accept her for what she is. The same understanding and capacity to relate to others will be an essential ingredient in pastoral leadership.

The elder's leadership skill is shown in his conduct of the family affairs. Paul's argument is simple. If the preacher cannot lead his own family group, how can he lead a diverse group of personalities within a church. Probably the most revolutionary economist in all of history was Karl

Marx. His radical ideas for remaking the economic basis of society have toppled governments across the world. But we are told that he could not even cope with the economic needs of his household. He was always in debt and often took the bankruptcy law.

By Paul's criterion, Marx failed in the test of the family principle. Marx's endless scrawlings on economics may have been an elaborate compensation for his own inability in managing family finances. He who cannot balance the household budget cannot solve the economic ills of the world!

Paul also emphasizes the deacon's family background. He, too, is to be the husband of one wife and in control of his own household. Moreover, he gives a list of qualifications for the deacon's spouse.

In consideration of all that Paul says about the relationship of church and family, we must face the charge of people who feel that, although the church should be an ally of the home, it is too frequently its enemy. The argument commonly used is that the church makes such demands upon the lives of people that there is little time left for family togetherness. So much time is spent preparing for church, being at meetings, and fulfilling organizational obligations that there is no time left for family activity.

The assertion should make us stop and think. If the accusation is true it demands attention. We might start by inquiring about the nature of family togetherness. Is it just physical proximity? Does it mean a family sitting in a room and looking at themselves or being under the spell of TV's hypnotic eye? There is a distinct difference between proximity and togetherness.

"Family togetherness" refers to the feeling of belonging to a common enterprise—of doing things together. Getting dressed for church and driving down the highway can represent family togetherness. Arriving at the church and going off to activities geared to the appropriate age level of the individual can mean that in this joint activity each individual develops his own distinctive outlook. Sitting in the same pew in church on Sunday morning, the family feels this is *our* church, this is *our* pastor, and we are worshiping *our* God.

Some sociological studies have shown that there is actually a positive correlation between churchgoing and the stability of family relationships. The family principle in the church strengthens both the church and the family. When Paul speaks about the church, he calls it "the house of God," for it is where God lives.

The Church Principle in Family Life

Not only is the church to be like the family but the family is to be like the church. The family principle in church life is to have its counterpart in the church principle in family life.

The church principle is to be seen in *teaching religion in the home*. In the Old Testament it had been the responsibility of the father to teach religion to the children. In Timothy's home the father was not a Christian, but the Christian faith was taught by the mother and grandmother. The boy Timothy was carefully instructed, for Paul says, "From a child thou hast known the holy scriptures" (2 Tim. 3:15).

Most translators render this word scriptures as sacred writing. The word is used for characters of the alphabet.

In the Epistle to the Galatians Paul used the word saying, "Ye see how large letters I have written with my own hand." Guy Ho King interprets this verse by imagining the boy Timothy learning the alphabet by placing his finger on the Hebrew letters of "the scriptures." The earliest reading lessons were permeated with the knowledge of God. The acquisition of worldly wisdom went hand in hand with gaining the knowledge of God. In the early days of American life this was often so. *The New England Primer* and the *Blue-Backed Speller* were both filled with religious as well as secular knowledge.

The church principle in the home is also seen in *family worship*. The reference to knowing "the scriptures" from a child obviously included the practice of family worship, which was a vital part of Timothy's home life. Sociologists are reminding us of the fundamental place of rituals in family life.

The story is told of Grace Moore's returning to her hometown. She visited a friend of school days who had married a country boy. He was obviously overwhelmed by the presence of the illustrious guest. As they sat talking and waiting for lunch, he continually addressed her as "Miss Moore." Trying to put him at ease, the great singer said, "Why don't you just say Grace?"

Whereupon the man stood to his feet, closed his eyes and said, "For what we are about to receive we are truly thankful."

For him the rituals of life learned in early days still remained as an almost automatic reaction. Religious rituals in the home often gain new significance and are enriched as the child develops.

Conducting family worship is an art. Introducing the

church principle of worship into the family may take effort, but it can be done. Remember to keep it brief, for the attention span of children is short. Let the children participate. They may be tantalizingly slow and halting, but be patient. If the Scriptures are read, take time to explain what the passage means. Vary the process. Monotony will kill it.

F. W. Boreham, who has written forty books of the choicest Christian devotional material, says his abiding memory of childhood was a weekly session known as the "Hassock Hour." The children sat on hassocks as their mother read stories which always ended on a religious note of challenge. Carlyle speaks of "the greatest academy —a mother's knee." Dr. Boreham was in large measure the product of the church principle in his home.

The church principle of *evangelism in the home* is seen in Timothy's life. There was a certain contagion of religious experience with Timothy's family. Grandmother Lois was probably influenced in Jerusalem where she was converted and returned home to win her daughter Eunice. Eunice had so prepared her son Timothy that when Paul arrived the boy was ready for the experience of divine grace. These were all links in the chain. The important thing was that there was no missing link.

After the maniac of Gadara had been healed, he wanted to follow Jesus. But our Lord said to him, "Go home and tell what great things the Lord hath done for you." The home may present the very best opportunity for our evangelistic enterprise.

Whether it be in teaching, worshiping, or evangelistic effort, the church principle should pervade all of family life.

The Reflection of Religious Conviction in the Quality of Family Life

In the letters to Timothy, Paul maintains there is a direct relationship between religious conviction and the quality of family life. Discussing the "last days," when religion will be at its lowest ebb, Paul says that children will be "disobedient to parents" and "without natural affection." With the decline of religious conviction, "honor thy father and thy mother" is no longer seen as binding, and family life degenerates.

The decline of religious conviction also means that the home is used for ulterior purposes— "creatures worm their way into other people's houses." All types of people knock on doors, most of them hoping to gain something from the experience. Many seek to exploit the whole family for their own purposes. Writing to Titus, Paul warns of individuals "who subvert whole houses" (1:11). A home is a vulnerable spot.

Throughout the centuries the church has struggled to set up criteria by which an individual's faith could be evaluated. Some of the creeds of Christendom have been elaborately formulated in an effort to pin down as precisely as possible whether an individual has the correct religious convictions.

Paul presents a most unusual idea when he says, "But if any provide not for his own, and specially for those of his own house, he hath denied the faith, and is worse than an infidel" (1 Tim. 5:8). True Christian faith produces family loyalty.

During the Reformation a peasant named Hans Ber rose from his bed at night and announced to his wife that in order to serve God he must leave her and the children. In response to her pleadings he responded, "Dear Wife, harry me not with the things of time. God bless thee. I will from hence that I may learn the will of the Lord." According to Paul's criterion, he was denying the faith by not providing for his family and was worse than an infidel.

Church and family go hand in hand.

10
The Mobile Family

Likewise greet the church that is in their house (Rom. 16:5).

Americans are on the move. This is not new, they always have been. Their forebears were adventurous spirits who left their well-established homes in Europe and sailed across the Atlantic in search of new ones. Arriving in the United States, they were not satisfied to settle on the eastern seaboard. They moved with the advancing civilization toward the West, with its free land and new possibilities. Many historians and sociologists believe the frontier spirit is an important factor in the development of the distinctive character of Americans.

The frontier movement was a search for wealth and adventure. When the desired situation was reached, the frontiersman became a settler who worked on his land and helped to build its value so that it might, in turn, be passed on to his children. It could be imagined that as the movement spent itself Americans would have been willing to settle down and "stay put."

However, with the advent of the twentieth century, with its rapid industrialization, improved communication, and remarkable transportation facilities, there came a mobility of which our ancestors never dreamed. It has been estimated that one American family in five moves each year.

The minister of a church in any town of moderate size will tell you of the number of people who come and go from his church membership. This moving, mobile, fluctuating population is a unique phenomenon of the twentieth century and has helped to bring into many lives strange experiences and sociological problems.

Though people on the move have the privilege of travel, change, and variety, the home has been one of the most tragic casualties of this mobility. When people grew up in a little community in which they were known, married and set up a family, there were community pressures which tended to keep them together. The new mobility has removed these pressures, and a fractured family life has been one of the debits.

It is not inevitable that the home should be a casualty of mobility. Confirmation of this comes from a biblical incident concerning Aquila and Priscilla, who moved around the world, yet maintained a magnificent Christian home. Born in Pontus on the Black Sea, these two young people, a Jew and Jewess, probably met in the services of the synagogue. After marriage, they fell under the spell of the big city and concluded they could better make their fortune in Rome, the capital of the mighty Roman Empire. Once in Rome, they set up their business in the textile trade. But it wasn't long before the rod of the Roman Empire fell upon them—an order from Emperor Claudius for the expulsion of all Jews from the city. They were compelled to sail across the Mediterranean to Corinth, where they had a series of experiences that led them to become Christians. The next move was to Asia

Minor where they settled in the city of Ephesus. From Ephesus they traveled to Rome and became the spearhead of the infant Christian movement. Some seven years later, in the last writing of the New Testament, they were back in Ephesus again. This couple illustrated that a Christian family can stay together, despite changing circumstances.

Woman's Place in a Christian Home

The names Priscilla and Aquila are mentioned six times in the New Testament. Priscilla is placed before Aquila on four occasions, even though Priscilla is the woman and Aquila the man.

The placing of the woman's name first has attracted the attention of biblical scholars. Sir William Ramsay suggests that Priscilla was of higher rank than her husband, her name being that of a good old Roman family. Conybeare and Howson[1] speculate that placing Priscilla before Aquila conveys the impression that she was the more energetic. She may have been the better "man" of the two.

The order of names is all the more remarkable when ancient literature is read, and the inferior position of women in the ancient world is observed. An example of this attitude is seen in the ministry of Jesus as he talked with the woman at the well. When his disciples returned, we are told that they "marvelled that he talked with the woman" (John 4:27).

The orthodox Jew had been taught that women were inferior creatures; and the pious Pharisee, who represented

---

[1] W. J. Conybeare and J. S. Howson, *Life and Epistles of the Apostle Paul* (New York: Thomas Y. Crowell Co., n.d.).

in many ways the most learned branch of the Jewish religion, lifted up his voice in prayer and thanked God that he was not a Gentile, a leper, nor a woman.

But Jesus, born of woman, brought a message of the equality of women. The apostle Paul, alleged by many to be a woman hater, took up the theme in his letters. He enunciated the great Christian truth that there is neither male nor female in Christ Jesus. Like so many other of Christ's social ideas, it has taken centuries for this to permeate society. It was not until near the end of the last century that woman's rights were recognized. The privilege of voting only came to women after years of turmoil and strife.

The church has been slow to implement the idea of the place of women. A century ago a young woman of the Church of England wrote to Arthur Stanley, the dean of Westminster, "I would have given her [the church] my head, my hand, my heart. She would not have them. She told me to go back and do crocheting in my mother's drawing room." Fortunately, this woman refused to go back and crochet. One of the outstanding women of the ages, Florence Nightingale accomplished what she did not only against the blundering officialdom of her day but evidently against the wishes of her church.

Woman's service for Christ has been very slowly recognized by society. Is it not strange that women who were not allowed to have a voice in the affairs of their church at home were permitted to travel to the far corners of the earth to preach the gospel? One church leader, contemplating the preponderance of women who volunteer for missionary service, has remarked that in Isaiah's day the prophet said, "Here am I, send me." In contrast, it seems as if the male of our day says, "Here am I, send my sister."

I don't think I ever realized the importance of the Christian concept of womanhood until I was in a Mohammedan country. I was being entertained in a Moslem home. All of the family were present. The mother sat at the head of the table with her sons on one side and her sons-in-law on the other. As the meal progressed, I discovered that the daughters and daughters-in-law were waiting in the courtyard. The mother was only present because the death of her husband had made her head of the house. At the conclusion of the meal we moved into a nearby room. As I peeped back, I saw that the daughters and daughters-in-law had rushed in and were eating the food left by the lordly men.

Contrast this with the modern American home. The position of women is one of the logical consequences of the impact of the Christian faith. As the Pilgrim Fathers developed and enlarged their Christian concepts, women were allowed to occupy their rightful place in the development of national life.

The battle of the sexes is over and done. In many instances the women have emerged victorious. Ashley Montagu has written a book called *The Natural Superiority of Women*. Unfortunately, for too many, being equal has come to mean being male or masculine, and women have lost much of their real power in the home and the community.

The Bible has revealed that the differences of the sexes are meant to be complementary, as each makes a distinctive contribution. A danger we face today is that the American male may become too feminine and the American woman too masculine. Carl Sandburg's biography of Abraham Lincoln tells the story of the young Lincoln's composing a wedding song for his sister. It was called "Adam and Eve's Wedding Song." Mr. Lincoln was obviously a greater statesman than a poet, but the sentiment of his poem is the important thing. The last three verses read:

> The Woman was not taken
>   From Adam's feet, we see,
> So he must not abuse her,
>   The meaning seems to be.
>
> The Woman was not taken
>   From Adam's head, we know,
> To show she must not rule him—
>   'Tis evidently so.
>
> The Woman she was taken
>   From under Adam's arm,
> So she must be protected,
>   From injuries and harm.[2]

Obviously, Lincoln had been reading Matthew Henry's Commentary, which says that "the woman was made of a rib out of the side of Adam; not made out of his head to rule over him nor out of his feet to be trampled upon by him; but out of his side to be equal with him, under his arm to be protected, and near his heart to be loved. The complementary aspects of husband-wife relationships are to the fore.

Outside of Ponca City, Oklahoma, stands a remarkable piece of statuary—a large bronze of the pioneer woman.

---

[2] Carl Sandburg, *Abraham Lincoln* (New York: Harcourt, Brace & Co., 1926), p. 53.

Clad in her long dress, poke bonnet, and button boots, she is striding across the prairie. Her left hand is holding that of her small boy, and in her right hand is a well-worn Bible. Sensible to the responsibility she has to her children, with faith in her heart and a willingness to risk with her husband all the hardships of the frontier, the pioneer woman typifies the place of a woman in the Christian home.

In Christ Jesus there is no place for a masculine superiority which overlooks the gifts given by God to woman as well as to man.

The Church in the Christian Home

Paul's father had insisted that he learn a trade, for the rabbis taught, "He who does not teach his son a trade, teaches him to be a thief." Aside from his studies in a Jewish school, the boy Saul spent much time learning to work with the haircloth supplied by the goats in his native province.

The wonderful system of roads built by the Romans opened the way for movement through the Empire, and travelers needed tents in which to sleep at night. Conybeare and Howson [3] describe this scene so familiar to the eyes of the boy Saul. At night there would be an encampment of tents of goat's hair or cilicium with a blazing fire in the midst. Horses were fastened around, and in the distance the moon shone on the snowy summits of Tarsus. The young man Saul had watched with pride as travelers haggled in the market place to purchase the tents which he had made, but love of books drew him from his tents to academic studies at the feet of Gamaliel.

_____
[3] *Ibid.*, p. 53.

Nevertheless, he was destined to have cause many times over to give thanks for the craft which his father had taught him as a boy.

Paul followed a well-designed plan of attack in his visits to great cities of his day. His first objective was the Jewish community. Arriving in Corinth, Paul was faced with the necessity of maintaining himself, so he looked around for work. His craft led him to seek employment in the tent-making establishment of the Jew and Jewess, Aquila and Priscilla. While working beside them, he applied not only a stitch in time but also placed one in the fabric of eternity, as he spoke to Priscilla and Aquila with such earnestness that they were converted.

The workroom took on a new atmosphere as they cut, stitched, and fitted the tent panels and talked fervently about the good news of the gospel of Christ. Customers came to buy but remained to pray. In the evenings, bales of cloth were pushed to one side and neighbor and visitor sat around on the workroom floor, while Paul poured out the gospel message.

He may have dramatically pointed to the tents in various processes of manufacture and contrasted for his audience the frailty of the human body with the permanent habitation God had prepared in the heavens. It may be that he warned them, as he did when writing to the Philippians, by speaking of death as "striking one's tent." In any case there was an excellent response to his message and many important Corinthian people were won to Christ.

When Paul felt that his work in Corinth was finished, Priscilla and Aquila packed their belongings and accompanied him to Ephesus, where they set up their tent-making establishment. Once again their home became a church, as believers gathered to fellowship and propagate the gospel of Christ. Paul, writing back to the Corinthian church, says, "Aquila and Priscilla salute you much in the Lord, with the church that is in their house" (1 Cor. 16: 19). When Paul left on his preaching journey into Galatia and Phrygia, Priscilla and Aquila continued to have church in their home, as well as attending the local synagogue.

Later, Paul planned to go to Rome. It may be that in planning his strategy he wrote to Priscilla and Aquila, urging them to move to Rome to help prepare for his coming. Despite the dangers involved in returning to a city from which they had been expelled, to Rome they went! When Paul wrote to the Roman church, he was able to send greetings to Priscilla and Aquila and also added, "Give my love to the little church that meets in their house" (Rom. 16:5, Phillips).

One sabbath there was a visiting preacher in the Corinthian synagogue. His name was Apollos. With fervor, skill, and boldness he told the assembled company the message of John the Baptist. After the service was concluded, Priscilla and Aquila invited the brilliant preacher to come and visit with them. Here they tactfully told Apollos that John was just the Forerunner, who had said of Jesus, "Behold, the lamb of God which taketh away the sin of the world."

The gifted young preacher rejoiced in the gospel message, listened with undivided attention as husband and wife expounded the truth of the gospel. He continued to question them until he understood the full implication of the message. Apollos now started out on a new mission ministry into Asia and became an outstanding evangelist of the early church, second only to Paul, all because of the faithfulness of Priscilla and Aquila.

There was a church in the home of Priscilla and Aquila. There should be a church in every Christian home, not in the sense of a fully-fledged organization, but in the sense that wherever two or three are gathered together in Christ's name, there he is in the midst. On the wall in some homes, perhaps over the breakfast table, hangs a little plaque, "Divine worship conducted here daily." This is as it should be.

The Christian faith has always made much of the home. One writer has indicated that on the day of Pentecost the Holy Spirit came upon the believers as they were gathered in a home. So the church was inaugurated within the confines of the walls of a Christian home. Possibly the most dramatic story Jesus ever told to describe a man's contact with God had to do with a boy's returning home. When Jesus wanted to speak about the ultimate goals toward which Christians are pressing, he said, "In my Father's house are many mansions."

The Possibilities of the Heroic in Christian Homes

Priscilla and Aquila were probably very ordinary people. It may be that neither ever preached a sermon. It could be that all they did was sit around and talk with people. But their home was a tremendous influence, and they had a sense of the overshadowing power of God. They were able to see that all of life was part of a divine plan.

The long trip from Pontus to Rome, with its anticipations of success and permanence, was followed by the catastrophe of the wrath of the Roman Empire and their expulsion from the city by Claudius. Corinth offered a new place to live, but after a series of adventures they moved to Ephesus. Through it all they saw the guiding hand of God. For them the events of life were overshadowed by purpose.

There is one incident of which we know nothing except when Paul speaks of it in the epistle to the Romans. Of Priscilla and Aquila he says, "for my life [they have] laid down their own necks" (16:4). What did this represent? We do not know. Perhaps there was a raid on the house. It may be that the Roman soldiers seized Paul, and Priscilla and Aquila said, "Don't take him, it is our church; we set it up in our house. Take us and let him go." So it could be that the soldiers released Paul and took Priscilla and Aquila instead. Paul says that all of the churches of the Gentiles were thankful for Priscilla and Aquila's risking their lives for him.

In our day and age we may need a new concept of the heroic. Inviting someone for a meal and trying to speak a word about Christ may not appear to be very heroic, but it is all-significant in God's service. Using our homes in this way may be one of our greatest services to God.

We have already noted that Jesus spoke about heaven as home. God wants all his creatures to share his hospitality. During World War II in Australia a father and son had an argument. The father ordered the son to leave home. The boy left. The family suspected that he had volunteered for service in the army, perhaps under an assumed name. Shortly afterward, large bodies of troops were sent overseas to the European front, where many were captured or lost in action. Communiques spoke often of men "missing, presumed killed." The family thought the boy might have been in this category, but they were never sure.

Each evening the mother continued a custom of the years. Whenever the children stayed out late she put the key to the front door under the mat just outside. As she put the key under the mat, she explained to a visitor, "We always did this whenever the children stayed out late. If he ever returns and looks under the mat he will see the key and know we want him back."

God's latchstring is always out. He wants men and women to come home. He can give them the empowerment of his spirit so that they can realize the heroic in their lives. In turn, they can have some little part in setting up a church in their homes.

Appendix

Friday

7:30 P.M.—Family Banquet
Subject: "The Family in a Modern World"
Arrange for Juniors and lower age levels to have an activity during the talk. Place cards on the table for questions which may be written out.

Saturday

7:30 A.M.—Men's Breakfast
Subject: "The Facts of Life for Fathers"
This could be sponsored by the Brotherhood.

7:30 P.M.—Parents' Meeting
Subject: "How to Talk to Your Children About Sex"
Serve pie and coffee to conclude the meeting.

Sunday

10:00 A.M.—A combined gathering of all the Intermediates and Young People (after the records have been taken).
Subject: "The Developing Love Life"

11:00 A.M.—Family Dedication Service
Subject: "The Family, the Laboratory of Life"
Families sitting together in church. After the message have dedication service.

6:30 P.M.—Training Union Hour
Subject: "Compatible or Combatible?—Husband and Wife Living Together"

All married couples to meet in assembly after records have been taken.

7:30 P.M.—Evening Service
Subject: "The Family Meal—Bickering, Bedlam, or Blessing?"